THINK WITHOUT LIMITS:
YOU *CAN* SPEAK WELSH

By the same author:
Social Context and Fluency in L2 Learners (2007)

think without limits:
you CAN speak Welsh

Lynda Pritchard Newcombe

First published in 2009

Published with the financial support
of the Welsh Books Council

ISBN: 978–1–84527–262–3

Cover design: Sian Parri

Published by Gwasg Carreg Gwalch,
12 Iard yr Orsaf, Llanrwst, Wales LL26 0EH
tel: 01492 624031
fax: 01492 641502
email: books@carreg-gwalch.com
internet: www.carreg-gwalch.com

'If you think without limits,
have the courage to try,
and the determination to see your goal through,
anything is possible.'

Caroline Hamilton,
the record-breaking polar explorer and motivational speaker.

This book is dedicated to the memory of my parents,
Llewelyn and Abigail Pritchard

Acknowledgements

Students in the Adult Welsh Language Project (AWLP) in Cardiff gave willingly of their time to take part in a pioneering venture in Wales. They completed questionnaires, wrote journals and attended interviews and focus groups. Without them this book as it stands would not have been possible. Thank you all for your help. Your efforts may well help many *dysgwyr* in the future. Language learners from Cardiff and elsewhere, who did not participate in the AWLP project, have also helped immensely by providing language autobiographies and making perceptive comments. Many thanks to the *Cymry Cymraeg* interviewed at the National Eisteddfod in Cardiff in 2008.

Many tutors, tutor organizers, other professionals, language learners and friends in Wales and further afield have read parts of this book and have offered valuable insights. Naming each one would fill more than this page. I am very grateful to them all but I would like to single out Gwen Awbery, Steve Morris and Viv Edwards, who have given generously of their time in reading and commenting on drafts. Gwilym Roberts provided many useful details on the history of Welsh for adults, and I am particularly grateful for his constant encouragement and for his belief in the value of this book.

I am very grateful to Rachel Heath-Davies, Adrian Price and the staff at Canolfan Dysgu Cymraeg i Oedolion, Caerdydd a Bro Morgannwg for their co-operation and support. Special thanks too to my husband Robert for his constructive observations, statistical advice and unstinting support. Finally I would like to thank the editor, Jen Llywelyn, for her encouragement and valuable, practical comments, and of course Gwasg Carreg Gwalch for their interest in this book.

Contents

Foreword
Dame Tanni Grey-Thompson

Language and the ability to communicate have always been important to me – after all, how can you get your point across if you don't have the means to communicate?

To reconcile this with being Welsh, but not able to speak the language fluently has always been something that has sat uncomfortably with me . . . There were lots of reasons, which seemed valid at the time and excused the fact that I didn't. My mother was Welsh-speaking but my father was not. It wasn't seen as a fashionable thing to do when I was a child, and I remember being told that if I wanted to go to University, having Welsh on my CV wouldn't count as a 'real' language, and I believed all of them.

Speaking Welsh, not learning it, was something that I always wanted to do. Speaking a different language is glamorous. Learning it takes time, practice, and the ability to laugh at oneself a little bit, because in order to do it properly requires having a go, and not being worried when people speak back and you don't understand. I was never worried about doing that in French or German, but Welsh always seemed different.

Then there was a change in my life that made a difference. My mother passed away and the link with the language was gone. I had always hoped that she would teach my children to speak Welsh and I could do it at the same time! I then realised that this was not going to happen, and the only person responsible for making it happen was going to be me!

Reading Lynda Pritchard Newcombe's book made me feel that I wasn't alone. Reading about the experiences of others in their attempts to master the language helped me understand that there is no right or wrong, but that many of the feelings that others were going through were what made me scared of trying. And that was what made it OK to try again. What it also helped me understand in Welsh (which I was perfectly used to dealing with in sport) is that there is nothing wrong with trying and getting it wrong – the worst thing is not trying!

I can still read better than I can speak, but when I get something right in Welsh, even the most basic conversation, I feel really proud of myself. I feel that I have achieved something and it has pushed me to try more. It has encouraged me to try interviews (recorded, not live, but that is a goal for me) and the reaction I have found has been wonderful. Most people are happy that I have tried, and for me it has given me the confidence to try more.

I don't know if I will ever be fluent, although it is still a dream, but what I have also come to understand is that there are lots of words in the *English* language that I don't know the meaning of, so all I can be is the best I can. I will keep learning my vocabulary, and think about my grammar, and I shall see each new day as a stepping stone. But most importantly I will remember all those other people who are trying to learn, and remember that there are many ways to be Welsh.

Tanni Grey-Thompson

Did you know that:

- Welsh, one of the many minority languages of Europe, is spoken by one in every five of the population of Wales?
- After decades of decline Welsh is now experiencing a revival?
- More young people are learning to speak the language?
- Since the 1960s the numbers of adults learning Welsh have increased dramatically?
- In the academic year 2006/7 there were 29,643 enrolments on Welsh for Adults (WfA) classes?
- Many fluent learners are playing a major role in revitalising the language?
- Sadly many others give up learning for a variety of reasons?

Learning a second language as an adult, though rewarding, can be a challenge. Practising and using the language outside the classroom is even more of a challenge. This book looks at what happens to adult Welsh language learners – referred to in this book as *dysgwyr* – when they *use* Welsh in the community. Hopefully, the accounts of their experiences will motivate many more, who have lost their ancestral language, to learn it. Quite a number of learners are from outside Wales and their stories may inspire others, from England and beyond, to learn Welsh. Learners' stories are told 'warts and all'. Challenges, joys and disappointments combine to build an absorbing picture of what happens when adults practise and use Welsh in the community.

One of the aims of the book is to help learners and *Cymry Cymraeg* (first-language Welsh-speakers) understand one another better so that they can help each other in the fight to restore one of the oldest languages of Europe.

The book does not offer *the* solution to the difficultites involved in learning a second language for such a solution does not and probably never will exist. However, the tips and strategies for learners presented here should encourage those with sufficient motivation and a willingness to invest time in learning and practising to become fluent speakers. First-language speakers could also be motivated to help learners more effectively by catching glimpses of learners' perspectives on their experiences outside class.

Whether you are a learner, a first-language speaker, a Welsh tutor, a researcher or even a learner of a second language other than Welsh, you will find fascinating, stimulating and inspiring stories and viewpoints in the pages that follow.

Adult Learner

I'm stuck in the swamp of this complex language,
                                    Squelching
through idioms and unrecognisable words. A sludge
of negative verbs seeps
over my boots, while possessive pronouns leech
onto my legs. Irregular plurals buzz
round my head and threaten
to bite if I don't inflect
them right. I grab
at mangrove branches to try to stay
standing. But they turn out to be
adjectives that must follow
the nouns they describe, and break
off. Mutations – scaly crocodiles – lurk
as I flounder, sharp-pointed rows
of consonants snapping
in the dark. I long to ask
the way to the higher drier ground
of my own language – *Saesneg* . . .
                os gwelwch yn dda . . .
                            please . . .
But I'm determined to survive here –
I tear the anaconda from my tonsils,
refuse to let it squeeze
me silent.

                                    Susan Richardson, 2007

think without limits:

Chapter 1
Thinking Without Limits

A Struggle Worth the Pain

When Sandi Thomas, an American of Welsh descent, was learning Welsh in Aberystwyth she described the process as 'a struggle worth the pain' – though sitting in a warm classroom chanting a few phrases or practising with a partner, lazing by the fire at home learning some vocabulary, lying on the sofa watching *S4C*, listening to *Radio Cymru* in the car, practising with other learners in a cosy café or pub, chatting to first-language speakers on a country walk and even swotting up a few mutations sounds quite 'wimpish' stuff compared with the hardships endured by the polar explorer, Caroline Hamilton. As a motivational speaker Caroline has stressed that for anyone who thinks without limits and has the courage and determination to achieve a goal, nothing is impossible. Caroline and her colleagues sustained their motivation to reach the Pole despite hauling sledges in freezing temperatures, sometimes below minus 45° Celsius, infected toes, frozen equipment and major storms with winds of 90 mph that restricted them to their tent for days at a time.

Caroline Hamilton and Ann Daniels celebrate reaching the North Pole in 2002.

Now I am not belittling the effort expended on learning a second language. In fact I abhor titles such as *Welsh in a Week* or *German in Three Months*, as they may spawn unrealistic expectations, and I wonder whether Brian Church's book, *Learn Greek in Twenty-five Years*, a facetious look at language-learning full of lively banter, is closer to the truth. What bothers me is this. There were 29,643 enrolments in Welsh for Adults (WfA) in the academic year 2006/7 and there have

15

been over 20,000 enrolments each year since 1996, as well as many learners on web-based courses or learning with family and friends, but only a minority progress to fluency and use the language regularly in the community, many giving up on gaining only a smattering. That is fine if all they wanted at the start was to stay at the 'get by' level, the sort of level I am quite satisfied with for Spanish, Italian or Greek so that I can find my way around, order a meal or do some shopping. However, I do not think that is what the majority wanted when they began learning. Welsh learners are rarely tourists. They want to *speak* Welsh.

In the chapters that follow, the spotlight is on adult Welsh learners – *dysgwyr* – and their role in a rapidly changing Wales. Portraits of learners will appear, as articles and (auto)biographies written about, and by, learners in English and Welsh over the last forty years intermingle with Cardiff learners' comments in the Adult Welsh Learners' Project (AWLP). For the project, learners wrote diaries and journals, and attended interviews and focus groups, between 1998 and 2000. Other students in Cardiff wrote journals in 2006. Quotations from students all use first-name pseudonyms to preserve anonymity. All the quotes in Welsh are verbatim and appear 'warts and all', with no corrections. We will also hear from first-language speakers. At the National Eisteddfod in Cardiff in 2008 I interviewed eighteen Welsh-speakers from all over Wales to find out about their experiences speaking to learners. Five of these said they did not know any learners. These Welsh-speakers are also referred to by fictitious names.

Dysgwyr – who are they? Why are they learning? What have some learners achieved? We will be concentrating on what happens to *dysgwyr outside* class. What are the issues they face when trying to use Welsh in the community, the family and the workplace? What helps learners? What are their fears and anxieties? Some learners successfully develop strategies that help them survive on the long road to fluency, others give up when the pressures involved in using Welsh outside class overwhelm them. First-language speakers and fluent second-language learners have the potential to support learners, but do not always understand how to do so. Is there room for attitude change here? Do some first-language speakers need help to understand the issues many learners face when transferring classroom Welsh to the community?

Why you will be glad you have read this book if you are a *dysgwr*
Learning a second language is an exciting and exhilarating journey, and the point where fluency is within reach is particularly thrilling. However, like most journeys there are high and low points. If you are armed with the knowledge that others who have shared their experiences with you have survived the journey, it will help you persist during low periods. Tips from experienced learners and tutors will also stand you in good stead when the going is tough and thoughts of giving up may raise their ugly heads. Do not consider throwing in the towel (*rhoi'r ffidl yn y to* – 'putting the violin in the roof' in Welsh), though there are times when it may be impossible to use Welsh as much as you would like because of what life throws at you.

The wisdom gained by those who have gone before will help you to continue learning and practising until you are fluent. Mairi Higham, now a fluent second-language speaker who teaches Welsh to adults and has taught in a Welsh-medium school, has likened the process of learning Welsh to playing 'Super Mario' on a Game Boy, coasting along and then smashing into a wall and feeling that she would never get over it. Then she would receive a boost and be up and over the wall and coasting again – until she hit another wall.

Julie MacMillan, Learner of the Year 2007, also felt she had hit a brick wall on occasions and was not learning anything at all. But she later realised how much she had actually been learning without realising it. She decided that when in the company of a Welsh-speaker she would say everything she possibly could in Welsh and NOT revert to English. She recalls how it would take her such a long time to say, '*Helo, sut 'ych chi? Beth wnest ti heddiw? Es i i siopa yng Nghaerdydd.*' (Hello, how are you? What did you do today? I went shopping in Cardiff.) and thinking, 'This is ridiculous, I could have said it ten times over in English'. That is when determination kicks in. She remembers thinking, 'If I stick at it, it WILL get easier and I will be able to say it more quickly.' She was right – she became a fluent speaker within three years.

All the AWLP learners expressed such fluctuating feelings in their journals to a greater or lesser degree. Here are Philip's thoughts:

The time for evening class is approaching and I have the strong feeling that all the climbing up ladders that I've achieved has been replaced by a fall down a long snake. . . . Anxieties were unfounded once back in class with Lucy's encouraging guidance back into gear – although it's a fact that so much of what I've done since we started is lost from memory – I often have to hastily scan over previous material rather frantically for the right word, form etc.

And Cathy's: 'With my son's teacher – I forgot a few words of Welsh. I said 'assembly' instead of service. I felt stupid.' However, later in the week she wrote, 'The Welsh is coming back. On the phone with a friend two minutes about arrangement for our boys who are performing in St. David's Hall tonight. Fine.'

But later:

I was suddenly spoken to in Welsh outside church and failed to understand because I wasn't expecting it. I felt a bit stupid . . . [Then] success at last! A telephone conversation with Lucy. As she is a sympathetic teacher she has the knack of being able to draw my meagre Welsh resources out in some coherent manner. This really boosted my confidence again. Why is learning Welsh such an emotional see-saw of success and failure?

Even Kim, who wrote of many successful conversations with Welsh-speakers, described bad days: 'Had a bit of a "bad day" today speaking Welsh to Brian's teacher, could not seem to find the words, made mistakes – feel like I will never be comfortable in Welsh.'

Why you will be glad you read this book if you are a first-language speaker

In 1957 Islwyn Ffowc Elis wrote a novel, *Wythnos yng Nghymru Fydd* ('A week in the Wales of the future'), in which the main character is projected into two possible futures. On one of Ifor Powell's journeys Wales is a province of western England where an elderly character tells Ifor she has witnessed the death of the language; on the other journey the language is flourishing. In the same way one could project Welsh learners into two possible futures – one in which they are nurtured and the majority become second-language speakers, and the other where many cease using Welsh after leaving classes as they have become disheartened in their attempts at fluency.

Noragh Jones, a learner from Ireland, is probably right in commenting that 'Wales is littered with furtive, failed learners or possibly the not so furtive who claim they have tried or are still trying.'

In the fight to restore the language a good deal of credit has been given to the role of Welsh-medium schools, protestations, and the media, but the part played by adult learners has received little notice to date. Fluent learners are already contributing to the language fight, and probably even more could do so if they had more help and support.

Many of the problems Welsh learners face are common to learners of other languages, problems with first-language speakers using dialect and slang or speaking quickly, for example. However, there are many settings in which there is no common language, learning French in France or Portuguese in Portugal or Chinese in China, for instance, and as a result regular language practice takes place as part of daily life. In Wales this is not the case and there is no practical necessity to learn Welsh. The musician Phyllis Kinney commented in 1992 on her experiences of learning Welsh decades earlier: 'All the Welsh-speakers I met were bilingual so there was never any necessity to learn Welsh in order to be understood.'

Pamela Petro, a learner from the USA, reflecting on her experiences on an intensive course in the 1990s, commented in a similar vein:

> The fact of the matter is that the principality of Wales is buried beneath the verbal tonnage of English . . . It takes fierceness and mental blinkers to learn it by pretending that you and the person with whom you're practising really don't share another language . . . Whenever I try to practise Welsh in Wales I get only so far before English comes spilling in from all sides.

These and other issues will be discussed more fully as the book unfolds. If you are a first-language speaker, fluent second-language speaker or a WfA tutor you will find information in this book that will inspire you to work more closely with learners to help them become fluent Welsh-speakers.

Before turning to *dysgwyr*, however, I would like to say a word to those who may have just picked up this book and are flicking through, thinking they do not need it.

One reason why you think you don't need this book

'They all speak English anyway.' If that's your attitude take a few minutes to read the following paragraphs. And you may change your mind.

Why do people of all ages, abilities and nationalities line up to learn Welsh every year? For a variety of reasons: to restore a family language, to keep the language alive, to communicate with family and friends, to help children in a Welsh school, to use Welsh in the workplace, to follow the media, to read literature. Some say, 'It's fun.' Others say, 'I needed a challenge.' Yet others believe learning Welsh is a courtesy to the 575,640 of Wales' inhabitants who speak the language fluently today. Many learners could not give a reason for their desire to speak Welsh. You may say we are back to the original comment, 'They all speak English. All these learners could save themselves the trouble.'

You are forgetting, though, that one of the key reasons why people learn Welsh goes beyond communication; it is linked with issues of culture and identity. Languages open up new worlds where hidden riches call to be discovered and cherished. Many learners want to imbibe the language of their forefathers and feel they can only really belong to Wales when they are fluent in Welsh.

And do you realise that this is not just happening in Wales but all over the globe? Near home there is increased interest in learning Irish and Scottish Gaelic, and even restoring Manx and Cornish, languages that had ostensibly died as spoken languages. There has also been a surge of people learning the lesser-used languages of Europe, such as Basque, Sorbian (a Slavic language found in eastern Germany), and even in the restoration of dialects such as *Plattdeutsch* in Germany.

Luxemburgian, spoken by very few, is now held in higher regard, and the production of literature for adults in that language has grown considerably since the early 1980s, despite the high prestige in which French and German are held in Luxembourg.

Even North America, known for its widely held 'English Only' attitudes, has witnessed a renewed interest in preserving and promoting some of the threatened languages of the First Peoples. At the University of California, Martha Macri has set up a programme to promote Native American languages, while in Canada the First

People's Cultural Foundation runs an on-line programme to help preserve and revitalize the languages of aboriginal peoples. In New Zealand, where everyone speaks English, there is increasing interest in learning Maori. In the Caribbean islands of Aruba, Bonaire and Curaçao, where most inhabitants speak English, Dutch and Spanish, demand is increasing for courses in Papiamentu, a language that has evolved from a blend of Spanish, Portuguese, Dutch, English, African languages and the language of the indigenous people. Papiamentu is not a second-class language, but the mother tongue of the working majority of the islands.

The issue is not one of communication but of sociability.

All over the world what is small, unique and special is adopting a greater place in the hearts and lives of many, despite – or perhaps as a reaction to – the increasingly prevalent global village environment in which we find ourselves. It could well be that the desire to revive a 'family' language and culture in societies whose social bonds in families and neighbourhoods are weakening, symbolizes a search for a community spirit lost to the majority in the twenty-first century. This is probably what has attracted many to the Welsh language. Pamela Petro, who has no Welsh roots, has hinted this was true in her own case and in the case of others known to her. 'The language gives you entry to a world that's disappearing everywhere else.'

Few people are aware of the serious plight of the world's languages. As many as one or two languages are lost each month. Languages are actually becoming extinct at a far faster rate than species of birds and mammals, a matter of great concern to linguists, anthropologists and UNESCO. There are those who argue that global communication would be easier with fewer languages. But the highly-esteemed linguist David Crystal likens the loss of a language to the loss of a people's identity, and believes the world would become bland if we all spoke the same language and thought in the same way. According to David, the intellectual health of the planet needs that kind of diversity to be creative. The death of a culture goes with the death of a language, and when a people adopt a more 'flourishing' foreign language, the sum of human knowledge diminishes. In Mexico, for instance, when some races adopted Spanish they lost the first-language terms for the plants they used in their everyday lives, and over time they could not remember to what uses such plants had been put.

The revitalised state of Welsh, together with languages as dissimilar as Basque, Faroese, Maori and Inuktiut, shows that it is possible to reverse the fortunes of endangered languages. However, preservation is still an up-hill struggle. Mrs Marie Smith-Jones, the sole native speaker of the Eyak language in Alaska, gained a global reputation for activism in preserving her heritage until her death in January 2008. Mrs Smith-Jones had been the last surviving Eyak since the death of her sister, Sophie, in 1992. This prompted her to begin campaigning on behalf of the region's indigenous people. She worked with linguists at the Alaska Native Languages Centre in compiling an Eyak dictionary and grammar guide and twice addressed the United Nations on the subject of peace and the preservation of indigenous languages.

In previous centuries a variety of factors including residential schooling, official oppression and even genocide brought about language decline and extinction. Causes in the twenty-first century are less dramatic but may be just as damaging: migration from a traditional area to a city, in-migration by speakers of a dominant world language, or the loss of confidence that occurs when lesser-used language speakers are exposed to mass media in powerful world languages such as English, as happens in Wales.

At the end of the nineteenth century Eliezer Ben Yehuda, a Polish Jew from Lithuania, was determined that the Hebrew language should live again. In October 1881 he arrived in Palestine. On the way he had written 'Today, we are speaking other languages; tomorrow we will be speaking Hebrew.' At the time it was generally accepted that

Eliezer Ben Yehuda (1858–1922), who determined to keep Hebrew as a spoken language.

Hebrew had died as a *spoken* language centuries earlier. One hundred years later 3 million Israelis were speaking Hebrew. Eliezer, moved by the novel *Daniel Deronda* by George Eliot (whose roots, incidentally, were in north-east Wales), was the pioneer who triggered this revival of Hebrew. Despite much derision, he decided, on the birth of his first child in 1882, that the Hebrew language alone would be spoken in his home. Thus his son became the first child for over 1500 years to have Hebrew as his mother tongue. One day a man stopped Eliezer on a Jerusalem street:

> 'Excuse me, sir. That language you two talk. What is it?' he asked in Yiddish.
> 'Hebrew,' Eliezer replied.
> 'Hebrew! But people don't *speak* Hebrew. It's a dead language!'
> 'You are wrong, my friend,' Eliezer replied with fervor. 'I am alive. My wife is alive. We speak Hebrew. Therefore, Hebrew is alive.'

The late Chris Rees, former director of Canolfan Dysgu Cymraeg i Oedolion, Prifysgol Caerdydd (Cardiff University's Centre for Teaching Welsh to Adults), was inspired by Eliezer's determination, and as well as initiating the intensive Welsh courses for adults based on the Hebrew system, he was eager to instil the same spirit of determination in Wales.

The revival of Welsh, and the place of adults learning the language, are, then, all part of a larger global picture. The late Gwynfor Evans, the first Plaid Cymru MP, commented in 1974 that the Welsh language is 'a bulwark' against the 'insipid uniformity of today'. How much more is this so in the twenty-first century global village? The world is slowly waking up to the gravity of the situation and Wales is becoming a leading light in inspiring other nations. In the mid twentieth century Welsh was under serious threat and its very existence in the twenty-first century was in question. The language has, however, made a remarkable comeback.

Mark Abley, author of *Spoken Here: Travels Among Threatened Languages*, concedes that languages, just like species, have lived and died in the past, but he believes that what we are seeing in the world today is entirely, hideously unnatural. Without intervention only about 10% of languages will survive by the end of the twenty-first century. Mark, like David Crystal, stresses that when a nation loses its language it often loses its culture and its heart. A world where everyone speaks Mandarin, Spanish and/or English and where the main fauna are rats and crows would not just be a poorer, less diverse place but a place where people have lost their identities, hearts and wills.

So it is not just a case of 'They all speak English anyway', is it?

Before we look at Welsh learners, the challenges they face and the part they are playing in restoring the language, I think it would be a good idea if I told you my story about learning Welsh.

Would you like to find out more?
Mark Abley, *Spoken Here – Travels Among Threatened Languages* (Heinemann, 2003)
David Crystal, *Language Death* (Cambridge University Press, 2000)
Islwyn Ffowc Elis, *Wythnos yng Nghymru Fydd* (Gwasg Gomer, 1993: an adaptation for learners in the *Cam at y Cewri* series)
Caroline Hamilton, *To the Pole* (Virgin, 2001)

Chapter 2
Learning to speak Welsh – my story

When did it begin?

Fans of C.S. Lewis' Narnia stories often disagree about the first book in the series. The first book Lewis wrote was *The Lion, the Witch and the Wardrobe*, but the birth of Narnia actually took place in *The Magician's Nephew* written some time later. Similarly it is difficult to place the beginning of my Welsh-learning story, which in one sense began eighteen years ago in New Zealand, but on another level began in the south Wales valleys in the 1950s.

Anyone who has attended a creative writing course will know that good stories have a beginning, middle and an end. This is not the case with language learning, where there never can be an end as there is always more to discover. Learning a second language has been likened by many learners to climbing a mountain. However, it is a mountain without a peak. Language-climbers enjoy the views but never reach the top as more idioms, more literature, and customs and culture bound up with the new language, are always coming into view. My story therefore has two beginnings, one middle and no end.

Ydw – rwy'n siarad Cymraeg – Inspired by a New Zealander

'Look, there's a dragon on the door!' said Robert excitedly.

'Not a Welsh dragon?'

'Yes, look, in the centre.'

Sure enough there he was standing proudly in the centre of the glass door, not the Maori *taniwha* but – *Y Ddraig Goch* (The Red Dragon).

'Am I dreaming all this?' I asked myself. Twenty-four hours in the air may cause you to mistrust your own judgement. The year was 1990 and we had stepped on to Southern Hemisphere soil for the first time two hours earlier. Following the welcome force-feeding of blueberry muffins and other delights by Robert's doting aunt and uncle, we set out for the local camera shop in Howick, an attractive suburb of Auckland, twelve miles from the city centre. We did not expect to find a great deal of Welsh influence in New Zealand, particularly in North Island. The Welsh tended to flock to North America, Australia and the Welsh-speaking colony of Patagonia in Argentina. Apart from John Gronow, an explorer from Pembrokeshire who named several areas in South Island after places in Wales, Welsh influence is not extensive. Hence, our surprise when we spotted *Y Ddraig Goch*.

We entered the shop to be greeted by a cross between Max Boyce and your average Welsh rugby player. It was obvious that Max was responsible for the emblem. He had Welshness written all over him. I asked Max where he came from originally and he replied Pontypridd. Only twelve miles from my home town, Merthyr Tydfil! I used to spend a lot of time in Ponty market years ago, I volunteered, and my parents used to take me to the open air swimming pool in Ynys Angharad Park.

Max was suitably impressed. *'Dych chi'n siarad Cymraeg?'* (Do you speak Welsh?), he asked boisterously. I was mortified. Max had touched a raw nerve and I was alarmed to have to give an account of my Welsh–speaking ability on the other side of the earth. I went into a lengthy explanation of how I learned Welsh in school but how it was very different to the Welsh spoken in the community . . . it was taught using the Grammar Translation method concentrating on reading and writing . . . therefore pupils usually lacked confidence in using the language with first-language speakers outside class . . . I told him I could sing Welsh songs and hymns, recite chunks of the Bible and poetry in Welsh and I had even read Welsh novels. However, I felt I would redeem myself in his eyes only by saying that my father, a first-language Welsh-speaker, had endured 'Welsh Not' attitudes at school. I announced proudly that my ancestors on my maternal side came from the Gwendraeth Valley, and my great-grandparents on my paternal side from Anglesey, both Welsh language strongholds.

Max yawned, clearly bored. 'What are you guys intending to do in New Zealand?' he asked in English. I breathed a sigh of relief and Robert gave him a résumé.

When I arrived home in Wales I enrolled on an intensive Welsh course. After a few sessions I began to speak some Welsh. All the school, family and chapel vocabulary came flooding back, and now, armed with knowledge of the more informal speaking registers, in particular the verbs, I began absorbing the language and using it at every opportunity. I studied hard, practised speaking, watched *S4C*, listened to *Radio Cymru* and read articles and books. I even started reading books and magazines that some first-language Welsh-speakers claimed were too difficult for them to understand fully. If Max could keep up his Welsh in New Zealand, surely I could learn to communicate in Welsh in Wales. After eighteen months I passed examinations, but these were not important compared with being able to communicate fairly fluently with Welsh-speakers at last. Oliver Davies, in the book he co-edited with Fiona Bowie, *Discovering Welshness* speaks for many from a similar background to mine when he writes:

> How could we ever claim to be one of 'them' when what made them 'really Welsh' was precisely that language, which we did not know? Welsh – those familiar but incomprehensible words – seemed an unbridgeable barrier between what they were and what we were: their fate and ours . . . I seemed to be becoming 'really Welsh' in that more precious way. I shall never forget the sheer thrill of answering the question, 'Do you speak Welsh?' in the affirmative for the first time, 'Yes, I do – *Ydw, rwy'n siarad Cymraeg.*' (Yes, I speak Welsh.)

When I returned to New Zealand three years later – a fluent speaker and a Welsh for Adults tutor – I set out triumphantly for the camera shop. Max was nowhere to be seen.

'Where is the Welsh-speaker?' I asked.

'Do you mean the guy from south Wales?'

'Yes, Pontypridd. I met him here a few years ago.'

'He's on holiday,' volunteered the assistant. 'He's a member of the Welsh society but he doesn't speak Welsh. He only knows a few Welsh phrases but enjoys using them.'

Max had really done me a favour but he never found out that he had been a catalyst in my Welsh learning experience. A hectic itinerary on the second trip to New Zealand meant I did not meet him again.

Beginning at the beginning

I was born in Dowlais, Merthyr Tydfil, south Wales in 1947. My mother, Abigail Pritchard (née Harris) understood Welsh but lacked confidence to communicate with my father, Llewelyn Pritchard, a first-language Welsh-speaker. I attended a Welsh chapel (which became a bilingual chapel) and learned Bible verses and hymns in Welsh, not always understanding some of the expressions. I learned Welsh in school, took part in a *cyd-adrodd* group in school *eisteddfodau* and sang Welsh songs in the choir. The school lessons rarely included oral practice and most of the time was spent reading, writing and translating with an emphasis on grammar and mutations.

Why then didn't I try to *speak* Welsh as a child and young person? This is a difficult question to answer. Like so many people who are brought up in Wales with some knowledge of the language from school and family I felt that a great deal was expected of me. This was *my* language that should be spoken correctly, not a language like German that I spoke quite fluently but in which it was acceptable to make mistakes, as a 'foreigner'. And certainly not like French, Spanish, Italian, Greek or Russian, areas where I have dabbled and where I think it is quite acceptable to gush forth inaccuracies and make silly gaffes. I imbibed the Welsh *anian* (ethos) to a degree but did not have a strong enough grasp of the spoken language to communicate fluently. The gap between the formal Welsh learned at school and the Welsh spoken in the local community was a hindrance to many in a similar position at that time. As a child I felt an oddity, since the other children at school and those I played with in the street did not speak Welsh, and at that time it was important to me to be like them. As an adult I wondered for many years about attending an intensive course but always procrastinated, unsure about what it would be like, how time-consuming it would be and whether I would ever be able to transfer my knowledge into 'street cred'. Ironically Max had given me the extra push I needed.

My family

My paternal grandparents and all my father's brothers and sisters were born in Llanllechid, Bethesda. My father was the only member of the family to be born in south Wales. My paternal grandfather, Edward Oliver Pritchard, was almost monoglot Welsh when he arrived in south Wales in the early years of the twentieth century and was never completely comfortable in English. My grandmother Mary Pritchard (née Jones) spoke Welsh with a north-Walian accent but was equally comfortable in English. She taught all her children to read Welsh before they attended school, which was a great advantage to my father since all his school education was through the English language.

My maternal grandfather, Aneurin Harris, whose family hailed originally from Cwm Gwendraeth, was bilingual. He had received limited education but was self-taught and a keen reader in Welsh and English. My maternal grandmother, Jane Harris (née Hughes), who was bilingual with limited reading and writing skills, was born and raised in Dowlais, though her family came from nearby Fochriw.

Despite her background, my mother was diffident about speaking Welsh as her parents spoke only English to her, though they spoke Welsh to her brothers. The neglect of language transfer was a common phenomenon in south Wales in her day. Parents often thought that concentration on English would give their children an advantage in life. However, in my mother's case, despite her being an avid reader, her parents did not encourage her to pursue her education, as they needed her at home to help caring for her brothers. Why not bring her up bilingually then? – a mystery she never could fathom.

Even though the older generation in my mother's day loved the Welsh language, a mindset developed that it was better for their children to be well-versed in English. In 1984 Dai Smith recorded the reminiscences of the writer, Gwyn Thomas, whose parents did not impart Welsh to him. 'My father and mother were Welsh-speaking yet I did not exchange a word in that language with them. The death of Welsh ran through our family like a geological fault. Places like the Rhondda were parts of America that never managed to get the boat.'

Though my parents were involved in many Welsh-language activities in the chapel, the *Cymmrodorion*, and took part in *nosweithiau llawen*, they rarely spoke Welsh to one another. This was partly because of my mother's hesitancy and partly because my father spoke north-walian Welsh. There was an attitude at that time amongst those who had not studied Welsh at school that their Welsh was not good enough and so was best left unspoken. This attitude is still prevalent today amongst Welsh-speakers who have received little formal Welsh language training. The main issue, I think, though, in my family was the difficulty in switching from one language to another with a close family member or friend. This is something that many learners have found problematic and we'll be looking at examples later in the book. Interestingly, when I was very young we had a cat, Timmy, and my mother spoke Welsh to him.

As my mother became less active, the more she listened to *Radio Cymru* and watched *S4C*. The media increased her confidence and inspired her to use Welsh as an elderly person. When I was learning, and doing homework, she could usually be relied upon to supply translations of vocabulary unfamiliar to me. It is never too late to learn a language or revive your skills if you are motivated to do so. As the pages of this book unfold it will become clear that motivation to succeed is often more important than any other factor.

They wanted to eat
The issue of family language loss is very close to my heart. If my great-grandfather, John Pritchard, a tailor, had not died prematurely, his sons, my grandfather, Edward Oliver, and my great-uncle, Elias Hughes, might have been able to pursue their education and may have remained in their beloved Gwynedd, still a Welsh-language stronghold. However, my grandfather had to leave school and work in the slate mines in order to help support the family in Llanllechid. Eventually strikes in the quarry forced him to bring his family to the south Wales valleys in search of work. Elias saved pennies for many years before he reluctantly left his widowed mother, his sister and five brothers to sail to New York in search of work. Both moves resulted in extreme damage to the future of the Welsh language in the Pritchard family. The presence of English in the south Wales valleys and the increasing influence of the media meant that though all Edward Oliver and Mary's children were fluent Welsh-speakers, their children and grandchildren had varying degrees of fluency in Welsh. However, in recent years the language has been restored to at least four Pritchard descendants who, like me, have built on their existing skills by attending courses for adults and are now fluent Welsh-speakers.

Elias and his German wife Lena had nine children and their descendants are spread all over the States. Although Elias' first language was Welsh and his English quite limited when he left for the States, it was difficult for him to teach his children Welsh. English dominated in his new home, and the children grew up speaking neither of their parents' mother-tongues.

Many years after Elias' death his grandson Llewelyn George Pritchard visited south Wales and asked his Uncle Iorwerth why his grandfather had left Wales, a country that 'honoured folks for being the best poet, the best singer and the best harpist.'

'It was quite simple,' Iorwerth replied. 'He wanted to eat.'

Llewelyn has since quoted Iorwerth's words to the House of Representatives as he continues to campaign for the rights of immigrant families to settle in the United States so that they too can improve their lot. Llewelyn's son, David Ashby Pritchard, one of the Microsoft moguls, has also echoed the words in his testimony on behalf of status for talented technical immigrants.

Although the American family have maintained an interest in 'things Welsh', attend Welsh societies, and some have visited Llanllechid, no member has any real grasp of the language. However, as interest in learning Welsh increases, both in Wales and in the States, and with the availability of web-based courses, it is quite possible that some of Elias' great-grandchildren may take up the challenge of learning the language of their ancestors.

Would you like to find out more?

Glyn Jones, *The Dragon has Two Tongues* (University of Wales Press, 2001)

Lynda Pritchard Newcombe, 'From Rachub to Riches' in *Ninnau*, Vol. 27 (3) (2002)

Chapter 3
Welsh is 'in'

Only rare species learned the so-called 'difficult' language
When Phyllis Kinney arrived in Wales from the USA in the 1940s, classes for adult Welsh learners were very thin on the ground and it was widely held that Welsh was such a difficult language it had to be learnt in childhood or not at all. By the time she returned in the 1960s, many Welsh classes for adults had been set up and were on the increase. Even in the 1980s, however, Lois Martin-Short came across the notion that adults learning Welsh could be wasting their time, '*Codai bobl eu hysgwyddau, yn dweud, "Wel, mae pawb yn siarad Saesneg rwan." Neu, "Iaith anodd i ddysgu ydy hi, mae'n well ei dysgu yn blentyn".*' ('People used to shrug their shoulders and say, "Well, everyone speaks English now." Or "It's a difficult language to learn. It is better to learn as a child".')

And in 2007 Jen Llywelyn commented, '"But isn't Welsh a difficult language to learn?" I've heard this so many times – and from the *Cymry Cymraeg* as well as learners.'

Hardly any adults learned the language formally until the latter half of the twentieth century. Those who did so were often of an academic or literary bent – such as the writers William Barnes, Gerald Manley Hopkins and J R R Tolkien and the politician, Enoch Powell – who were generally more interested in reading than speaking the language. Gerald Manley Hopkins claimed that the language and poetry of Wales, in particular *cynghanedd*, inspired his own poetry, and Sindarin, a language spoken by the elves in Tolkien's trilogy, The Lord of the Rings, was profoundly influenced by Welsh. Tolkien was fascinated by the language as a young boy when he saw names such as Penrhiwceiber on trucks in the Midlands. Later on a railway journey in Wales he said the Welsh words he saw were more appealing to him than any he had previously encountered, 'a flash of strange spelling and a hint of a language old and yet alive . . . it pierced my linguistic heart.'

In 1914 he shocked his Oxford contemporaries by spending money from a prestigious prize for English on John Morris-Jones'

Welsh Grammar. Despite his enthusiasm, however, he rarely visited Wales, as for Tolkien, examining pages of a medieval text was more powerful and satisfying than speaking the language with the locals.

Another man of letters who learned Welsh long before adult classes for learners mushroomed in Wales was the poet R S Thomas. The daughters of H D Owen, the minister at Manafon, in mid-Wales who helped R S Thomas gain fluency, still recall how difficult they found it to communicate with him when he visited their parents, because he used 'book Welsh'.

I want 'street cred'

In the 1960s greater emphasis on oral rather than written work in class helped produce learners who were able to communicate more naturally and acceptably with first-language speakers. The demand for adult classes in Welsh continued through the 1970s. There were 388 evening classes running in Wales teaching 5,189 adults by the academic year 1972/3, and 50 classes outside Wales teaching 570 students. But some students and tutors were dissatisfied and questioned how much was actually being achieved – were new speakers being produced or was there just renewed interest and goodwill towards the language? Trevor Vaughan who represented the local authorities on the University of Wales' extension board commented, 'I've been learning Welsh now for three years. I can say things like, *'Mae'r dyn yn cerdded'* (The man is walking) but I still can't understand people talking. What are you going to do for people like me? I'm on a plâteau and I can't get off it.' Such comments contributed to the decision by the University to investigate Welsh for adults courses and employ a research and development officer, Chris Rees, in 1974.

Wales inspired by Israel – rapid growth in numbers of learners

In the 1970s the pioneering WLPAN intensive courses, inspired by the ULPAN method used to teach Hebrew to immigrants in Israel, helped set in motion an astounding growth in the number of learners. The method used in Israel is the direct method, Hebrew through Hebrew, with very little grammatical explanation and extensive use of drills, games and dramas.

An intensive Welsh course for teachers was held in Barry College in 1966, but it was in 1973 that the WLPAN courses for the general public began. Chris Rees and Gwilym Roberts, both iconic figures in Welsh language promotion, ran the first WLPAN course at the *Urdd* Centre in Cardiff in 1973. Students attended five times a week in the evenings over a ten week period, together with a residential weekend at the *Urdd* centre in Llangrannog. Chris Rees, who was later called *Tad yr WLPAN* (Father of the WLPAN), prepared a skeleton syllabus, while an enthusiastic group of tutors, all of whom worked voluntarily, taught the sessions.

Chris Rees (third from left), known as 'Tad yr WLPAN' (the father of WLPAN), who set up the first WLPAN course in 1973.

Gwilym, the instigator of the once-weekly Welsh classes in Cardiff nearly ten years previously, was one of the tutors. He described the results as "staggering" as students learnt as much in ten weeks as people would normally learn in two years of weekly lessons.

When Chris Rees and Gwilym Roberts went to London to visit Mrs Eytan at the Education Department of the International Jewish Institute, in the early days of establishing Welsh WLPANIM, they expected to learn of some unusual teaching methods to account for the success of the Hebrew ULPANIM, as Mrs Eytan had had considerable experience as a *mora* (tutor) before moving to the UK. However, all she told them was that the ULPAN tutors used mainly

Students on the first WLPAN course in 1973.

chalk and talk and that a great deal depended on the enthusiasm and personality of the tutors.

In some respects the Welsh WLPAN was a pale reflection of the Hebrew model. The majority of students in Wales had worked all day before attending the WLPAN in the evening, thus sacrificing their leisure time to learn the language. In Israel it was commonplace for ULPAN students to have several months free from work at the government's expense to learn Hebrew. Despite this many now fluent Welsh-speakers trace their inspiration in learning back to attendance on WLPAN courses.

Research on WLPAN over the years has shown that the majority of students have benefited from the WLPAN method. However, it does not suit everyone. Some students do not like learning to say phrases before they see them, although many get used to this as the course progresses. Others would like more emphasis on grammar rather than conversation early on in the course. Yet others would prefer less stress on grammar. Some people consider that the methodology used does not take into account the fact that learners learn in different ways. You can read more about this in *Welsh in a Year!* by Jen Llywelyn. In September 2009, in response to research findings on the way adults learn, Cardiff University decided to allow

Welsh-language students to see the course materials before learning it in class.

Hilda Hunter and Caroline Williams in their book *Dysgu Cymraeg/Venturing in Welsh* have challenged the way WfA is taught. They call for smaller classes and would like far more error correction. The issue of fluency versus accuracy has been a bone of contention amongst scholars for decades. On WfA courses students are not usually corrected directly but the correct form is emphasised by the tutor and the student is expected to repeat it. When tutors were trained in the early days of WfA and WLPAN, Chris Rees stressed the importance of not making the learner feel uncomfortable by over-correcting. This could hinder the development of fluency. The keen learner, it was argued, would eventually learn the correct forms. Moreover, making mistakes when speaking is part of the learning process. If students wish to be corrected every time they make a mistake they should make this plain. However, in the earlier stages of learning, conversations will be rather contrived if there is too much emphasis placed on accuracy.

The Turning of the Tide

The Welsh WLPAN was born in an era when the fortunes of the language were changing. In 1962 Saunders Lewis delivered his historic radio address *Tynged yr Iaith* ('the fate of the language') warning that drastic action was essential for the language to survive into the twenty-first century. As a result of his appeal *Cymdeithas yr Iaith Gymraeg* (The Welsh Language Society) was founded and succeeded in gaining recognition for Welsh in many areas. The society was active in teaching the language to non-Welsh-speakers in the 1970s, as was the *Urdd Gobaith Cymru*, which held classes and summer schools regularly. The summer schools were particularly fruitful, and some fluent learners, the product of this time, are now prominent figures in Welsh life. Wyn and Christine James are prime examples. Wyn is a senior lecturer in the Welsh department at Cardiff University and the author of several books and Christine is a senior lecturer in Welsh literature in Swansea University.

WLPAN inspires barefoot tutor

Another student on a later WLPAN at the *Urdd* Centre in Cardiff,

Howard Miles from Tredegar, went on to teach a group of men at the local rugby club using the WLPAN material. Traditionally Welsh had been taught as a literary language and knowledge of the workings of grammar assumed. However, the WLPAN method, which stresses speaking and learning patterns, can be embraced by those with little educational background. Howard, a skilled manual worker in heavy industry, had no background in language learning and no teaching qualification or experience. He attended two WLPAN courses, one in Risca in addition to the Cardiff course, and subsequent weekly courses to improve his command of the language. He commends the WLPAN method as it enables students to retain language and use it to communicate after a short period of time. At the end of his thirty-week course most of his students could communicate in Welsh using all the tenses. Many of them continued to use Welsh after the course was over and some arranged for their children to attend Welsh-medium schools.

More than 'mildly interested'

Neil Caldwell, now a community regeneration consultant in Cardiff, is another example of someone who learned on the WLPAN at the *Urdd* Centre in the 1970s. Neil, who continues to use Welsh,

Gwilym Roberts, who ran the first ten-week WLPAN course in Cardiff in 1973, with Chris Rees.

described his experiences in *Discovering Welshness* in 1992:

> Like so many others, I began by attending an evening class. It was difficult to believe I would ever be fluent under this regime which seemed to cater only for the mildly interested . . . Being an all-or-nothing type, it didn't satisfy me. So I cleared the decks and signed up for an intensive ten-week WLPAN course at the *Urdd* Centre in Cardiff, under the irrepressible Gwilym Roberts. The strange thing was that, although this involved a total commitment of three hours a night, five nights a week, it was far easier and a great deal more fun that the once-a-week evening class. From the start I knew every evening was filled, so that my days were arranged to suit. I was immersed in the language to such a degree that it would whirl in my head during the day. On top of this, I got to know my disparate group of learners so well that we lost all inhibitions and fell about laughing at the least excuse! It was wonderful.

Neil felt that the emphasis on the spoken language, rather than grammatical forms, was a key factor in his success enabling him to achieve his aim of being able to communicate outside class.

A phenomenal growth

Over the decades, and particularly in the 1990s, the number of enrolments on Welsh courses provided by universities and local authorities, both intensive and non-intensive, grew at an astonishing rate to over 20,000 each year from 1996, with record enrolments of 29,643 in 2006/7. Many adults are also learning through distance learning programmes, on-line courses, with private and voluntary agencies, and with private tutors. In 2006 six further and higher education institutions were selected to become dedicated language centres to plan and deliver WfA provision. Over the same period there has been an increase in the number of Welsh learners outside Wales, in particular in the London area and the USA. In November 2008 the Open University offered its first-ever Welsh Course, CROESO L196, and were surprised by the response of 340 registrations, 163 of which were from outside Wales.

Many people learn Welsh in Patagonia, South America,
and come to Wales to practise.

Patagonia

Over the the last fifteen years there has also been an increase in the number of Welsh learners in Patagonia, some of whom spend time in Wales practising their Welsh-language skills. Patagonia is a particularly interesting case, as over the past twenty years there has been a radical change of attitude amongst those of Welsh origins. In the 1970s, in a radio broadcast in Patagonia, Professor Robert O. Jones lamented that he was witnessing the death of the language; but more recently he has expressed amazement at the new-found pride in the area's Welsh heritage, with even Argentinians of non-Welsh descent, such as Sandra de Pol, Welsh Learner of the Year 2001, learning the language. Robert warns, however, that the language is by no means safe, as the older generation (*y to hŷn*) who spoke Welsh as

---

Robert's top tip for learners

'Insist on using Welsh. The important thing is to move from the mother tongue, whether that be Spanish or English.'

Menter
PATAGONIA
a PWYLLGOR TIWTORIAID CYMRAEG Y GAIMAN

DEWCH I SGWRSIO

Pob Nos Fercher
20:30

Cyfle i ddysgwyr o'r Gymraeg gyfarfod ac
ymarfer yr iaith.
Croeso i ddysgwyr a siaradwyr o'r Gymraeg

Yn GWALIA LÂN, Y GAIMAN

Menter
PATAGONIA

*Menter Iaith Patagonia poster inviting people to
conversation practices every Wednesday night.*

their mother tongue are dying out. This is the view of Walter Ariel Brooks, a fluent Welsh learner from Patagonia, who works as a WfA tutor and researcher in Cardiff University. Walter thinks that learners are less fearful of trying to use Welsh in Patagonia than they are in Wales. However, as happens in Wales, many school children are educated in Welsh and then use their first language, Spanish, when playing with other children in the yard and at home. *Menter Iaith* are working in Patagonia at present to try to encourage learners to use the language more in the community.

Cŵl Cymraeg

Welsh is seen in a far more favourable light in Wales than it was half a century ago and it is sometimes viewed as 'cool' and fashionable to learn it. A student on a course at Aberystwyth remarked, 'Welsh is getting to be so "in" to learn that someday half of the people in Wales will speak Welsh. I'll be one of them too.'

Welsh has had a higher profile in the media of late. In 2001 an article on Wales appeared in *National Geographic*. It included a section on the author's experience on a Welsh for Adults taster course, which he evidently found quite challenging:

> 'Simon, do you want to try the first one?' asked our teacher. Carole couldn't have been nicer. But as I stared at the words Betws-y-coed, I began to get that sweaty feeling I remember from school

when the chemistry teacher would quiz us about the periodic table.

Following controversy on the use of Welsh on the reality television show, *Big Brother*, an article on the language appeared in the *Guardian* – and even the *Sun* included Welsh on its front page in support of Glyn Wise, the Welsh-speaking *Big Brother* contestant.

Welsh – a beacon of hope

Visitors from many different regions and countries have been impressed by Wales' political and linguistic schemes in recent years as the country gains reputation internationally for its role in promoting bilingualism. Indeed, Welsh has become a leading example of the reversal of language decline, which is quite remarkable in the light of the language status of its next-door neighbour. As the journalist, Mark Abley puts it, 'Modern English is the Wal-Mart of languages: convenient, huge, hard to avoid,' superficially friendly, and devouring all rivals in its eagerness to expand.'

In 2004 a Corsican television company filmed in a variety of locations in Wales; a TEFL lecturer in Japan, Marshall Childs, commended Wales' progress towards bilingualism; and a delegation of Iraqi Kurds, a group whose language has been greatly oppressed, came on a fact-finding mission to Wales. Probably the most encouraging of all comments is that of Peter Austin, head of the Hans Rausing Endangered Languages project in the School of Oriental and African Studies at the University of London, who believes that Wales is sending a lesson to many parts of the world when it comes to preserving language. The language is also enjoying recognition on the World Wide Web with over a hundred chat rooms in the Welsh language alone. David Crystal views the internet as a possible saviour of many endangered languages, as

The linguist David Crystal views the internet as a possible saviour of many endangered languages.

chat rooms and websites have made them appear 'cool' to many young people. He regards Welsh as 'a beacon of hope', as numbers of speakers are starting to increase, and he views the internet and chat rooms as major players in this revival.

Not a time for complacency

Despite the encouraging statistics and positive attitudes, however, there are still only a limited number of Welsh learners who attain fluency and become integrated in a Welsh-speaking community. Many do not finish courses, and some who do never use Welsh in their community. There are many reasons for this. Time is often a key factor as adults are usually constrained by employment and domestic responsibilities, and periods allocated for learning and practising may be limited. This is why many successful learners describe an intermittent pattern of learning, sometimes starting and restarting courses over long periods before they eventually become fluent. Bereavement, childbirth, illness, promotion, moving house are all factors that may cause learners to give up permanently or temporarily. Other factors are dissatisfaction with the tutor, the course material and the methodology used in class. Anxiety and lack of confidence can also be significant. However, one vital issue, and the main area of focus in this book, is what happens when learners try to practise and/or use Welsh with Welsh-speakers *outside* the classroom.

Helen Prosser, senior lecturer at the University of Glamorgan and a leading light in WfA, believes that learners could transform the linguistic situation in Wales, as it is possible for the committed to become fluent speakers in a period of two to six years. Bobi Jones, the first Welsh learner to become a professor in Welsh and a pioneer in the early WfA teaching movement in the 1960s, also thinks that adult learners are of vital importance in the fight to revive the language and culture of Wales. Adults *choose* to learn, Bobi argues. They vote, create attitudes, and can change the language of a household. While protestations and campaigns for language rights have been effective in the past, if there is to be a radical revival of the Welsh language, protestors should also consider giving more time to helping learners hold a conversation. The psychology of first-language speakers needs to change in this area if the battle for the revitalisation of the language is to be won. Welsh-speakers tend to transfer the problem to others, hoping that those in authority will change matters. Bobi believes that Welsh-speakers should be proactive in language revival by helping learners, giving them regular practice opportunities, rather than leaving this task to classes and voluntary movements.

In recent years numbers of adult learners have increased rapidly in areas such as Gwent and Glamorgan, and many make a contribution to the promotion of the language in the community and workplace. Geraint Wilson-Price has led a successful team in Gwent where regular Saturday classes for learners attract people from Gwent and beyond and have inspired many learners to progress to fluency. Traditional heartland areas such as Gwynedd, Carmarthenshire, Ceredigion and north Pembrokeshire, however, are losing many first-language speakers because of migration from the area and the language is losing ground there because of in-migration by English speakers, many of whom do not attempt to master the Welsh language. The language has received a serious battering in these areas, and is under threat because of factors such as village school closures, successive farming crises, the high cost of fuel and bankruptcies among small businesses. It is easier for learners to build on their language skills in these areas at present, as there still exists a community where it is possible to hear and use Welsh when conducting day-to-day affairs. However, far more learners will need to progress to fluency if they are to make a significant contribution in this critical situation.

If learners are to become integrated into Welsh society it is vital they realise that classes are only a foundation, a spring-board into the world of Welsh language and culture. However, they need to be highly motivated, enterprising individuals if they are to practise and use the language, particularly in areas such as south east Wales where there are few opportunities to speak Welsh in daily life. Such individuals do exist, however, and we will meet them later. As knowledge grows it must be combined with flexibility and determination. First-language speakers can play a vital role here in helping learners' progress to fluency – but often do not do so. Many first-language speakers feel uncomfortable with learners and do not know how to help, while others are conscious of their own limited skills, particularly if they have not studied Welsh at school.

I believe that anyone who becomes a fluent second-language speaker as an adult is doing something very brave, demanding patience, hard work and a humble yet determined spirit. Such individuals need the support of their tutors, classmates, family and friends and the first-language community. The main aims in the pages that follow are to help first-language speakers understand learners' needs and to encourage learners to persist when they become disheartened. Fluent second-language speakers have contributed to the fight of revitalising the language, and there is the

Students in an Open University tutorial at Reading practise speaking Welsh. The first OU Welsh course attracted 350 participants.

potential for increasing numbers of learners to become second-language speakers and contribute still further. Now let us look at some of the learners and why they are learning.

Would you like to find out more?
Richard Crowe, *Yr WLPAN yn Israel* (Canolfan Ymchwil Cymraeg i Oedolion, Aberystwyth, 1988)
Bobi Jones, *Language Regained* (Gomer, 1993)
Hilda Hunter and Carol Williams, *Dysgu Cymraeg, Venturing into Welsh* (Y Lolfa, 2008)
Jen Llywelyn, *Welsh in a Year!* (Y Lolfa, 2007)
Theodor Schuchat, *Ulpan: How to learn Hebrew in a Hurry* (Gefen, Jerusalem, 1990)

Chapter 4
Dysgwyr: Who are they and why are they learning?

The majority of learners are of Welsh origin and many of them, like me, are eager to restore a language not fully transferred to them by previous generations. Carl Clowes, a learner with Welsh roots who spent most of his childhood in England, has made a particularly significant contribution to learners' education. Carl established a Trust in 1978 and bought and renovated Nant Gwrtheyrn, a village of twenty-six quarry workers' houses on the Llŷn peninsula. It became a successful centre for language learning, and hundreds of people, as families or as individuals, visit each year from Wales and beyond.

Some learners are from outside Wales, and as the 1970s progressed, more students from England attended classes. Colin Pearce at Treforest commented, '*Sais wyf i, ac rwy'n gobeithio medru siarad Cymraeg gyda'r fferyllydd, clerc y banc a'r milfeddyg ym Mhontypridd, a dysgu ychydig o eiriau i Buster, y ci hefyd*' ('I am an Englishman and I am hoping to be able to speak Welsh to the pharmacist, the bank clerk and the vet in Pontypridd, and teach a few words to Buster, the dog too.')

Most students of non-Welsh origin are from other parts of the United Kingdom, though some hail from overseas and many of these are learning Welsh through their second language, English. Some of these are from Patagonia and only have a limited knowledge of English.

Many adults are learning in order to communicate with and help their children. Some learners, who have retired from full-time work, have grandchildren in Welsh-medium education, and are eager to communicate with them in Welsh and help with homework. Other learners in retirement have finally found time to fulfil a lifelong ambition in learning their ancestral language, while others are eager to socialise with Welsh-speakers.

Some of the latter are totally committed to the language and satisfied with nothing less than fluency. Some have made immense personal and financial sacrifices in order to achieve their goal. John Stiff, for instance, who had no opportunity to learn Welsh in childhood, gave up his job for a whole year in the 1970s to attend an intensive course. In the late 1990s Laura, one of the students in the AWLP, turned down the offer of a permanent post in England as she was so eager to continue learning Welsh.

Den and Ann Rees are prime examples of successful older learners. Following their early retirement in Gwent – one of the most anglicized areas of Wales – they attended an *WLPAN* course. Subsequently they became fluent Welsh-speakers, changing the language of their home from English to Welsh despite no family or educational background in the language. They now express themselves more fluently in Welsh than some first-language Welsh-speakers.

Another remarkable example of an older learner is Hilda Hunter who, in the year 2000, when she was over 80 years old, realised a dream she had cherished since her period in Aberystwyth in the 1950s and became a fluent Welsh-speaker. She published her autobiography in Welsh, *Dyfal Donc*, in 2006 and co-authored *Dysgu Cymraeg/Venturing into Welsh* with another fluent learner, Caroline Williams in 2008. And in the Learners' Tent at the National Eisteddfod in Swansea in 2006, 90 year old Helena Ann Jones was presented with a WJEC certificate to mark her success in the 'Sylfaen' examination.

Some learners are interested in following the media in Welsh; others are interested in Welsh culture and literature. Some have themselves made significant contributions to Welsh cultural life. Robat Powell, for example, a learner from Ebbw Vale, won the Chair at the National Eisteddfod in 1985 for writing an ode in *cynghanedd*, and Alison Layland from England, Learner of the Year in 1999, has won prizes for short stories and has published a Welsh-language novel. Lois Arnold, winner of the Learner of the Year competition in 2004, has also published a novel for learners. In 2005 Christine James, who learned Welsh as a second language in school, won the Crown for the best poem at the National Eisteddfod. Toni Bianchi, who was born in England, has won several awards for his literary work in Welsh, including the Daniel Owen Prize for fiction at the 2007 National Eisteddfod.

In 2005 Christine James, a second-language Welsh-speaker, won the Eisteddfod Crown for her poetry.

There have been many successful learners in the political arena. Jane Davidson, David Davies and the late Phil Williams have used Welsh confidently when speaking at the National Assembly for Wales; Janet Ryder, originally from the north of England, is now a fluent Welsh-speaker, and an assembly member for Plaid Cymru.

At the National Eisteddfod in 2008, I spoke to Emlyn, a first-language speaker, who expressed admiration for the politicians who had learned Welsh, such as Alun Pugh and Mike Bates, and actually use their skills in the work-place: it is not easy to use a second language at work when the subject matter becomes technical.

During the 1990s the numbers of courses for learners specifically geared to workplace needs increased significantly. These proved popular but often suffer from higher drop-out rates than other courses. Many students have also implied that despite their attendance on workplace courses provided by their employers, their main motive for learning is the wish to communicate in a variety of settings with Welsh-speakers.

A significant proportion of WfA tutors are second-language Welsh-speakers. Lila Haines, originally from Ireland, speaks for many: 'I believe that learners can make very good teachers because we know what difficulties are facing people who are learning.' Similarly, Angela Evans, originally from Yorkshire commented, 'I find that my own experiences of learning the language helped me to appreciate the difficulties my pupils experience. I have learned not to take anything for granted, and to put myself in their shoes.' Empathy with students is likely to reduce anxiety not only in the classroom but outside, because the adult learner who becomes a tutor has successfully transferred skills from the second-language classroom to the community and should therefore be able to inspire students to follow suit. First-language Welsh tutors are of course able to provide insights into the Welsh-language world which a tutor who has learned the language may not be so au fait with. Ideally if learners meet more than once a week it is of great benefit for them to have a mix of both types of tutor.

Some learners are in-migrants from other parts of the UK and elsewhere and many of these have become fluent and use Welsh regularly in the community and the workplace. A radio programme for learners, *Catchphrase*, for instance, featured Beverley Lennon from south London whose family originates from Jamaica. Beverley went on to teach Welsh as a second language and had her own show on Radio Cymru. Nushin Chavoshi-Nejad, a linguist from Cambridge, originally from Iran, whose first-language is Farsi, has learned Welsh and works as a Welsh for Adults tutor in south Wales. Wayne Howard, now a Welsh as second-language teacher in a Cardiff comprehensive school, is also from an Afro-Caribbean background. He learned Welsh while working full-time in the Cardiff steel works and bringing up his children, who attend Welsh-medium schools. Wayne's achievement is even more remarkable: he lives in Trowbridge, an area of Cardiff that has one of the lowest proportions of Welsh-speakers. The winner of the Learner of the Year competition in 2002, Alice Traille James, now lives in Crymych, but was brought up in London and her family originate in the Caribbean. Meinir, a first-language Welsh-speaker from Aberystwyth has encountered several learners from overseas who are learning Welsh through their second-language, English. She has noticed that they learn faster than those who are monoglot English and attributes this to the fact that they have already been through the process of acquiring a second language.

There has been a fundamental change in attitude since Charlotte Williams wrote of her childhood experiences in the 1950s and 1960s in north Wales: 'There was no conception of black Welsh.' Steve Morris, an experienced WfA tutor and researcher, has noted that it is no longer unusual to meet Welsh-speaking people born in other countries or members of ethnic minorities, who often have had little prior contact with traditional Welsh culture. This diversity is reflected in the many learners whose origins are overseas, from countries as diverse as Japan, Iran, Iraq, North Africa, Syria, Jordan, North America, Argentina, India, Germany, France, Switzerland, Luxembourg, Greece, Poland and the Czech Republic. At the National Eisteddfod in 2007, in a special session in Maes D (the learners' pavilion), Gwilym Roberts led a session where several overseas learners gave their stories when learning Welsh on stage to a packed audience. In 2008 at the National Eisteddfod four fluent learners from the USA and Argentina, who work through the medium of Welsh, described their learning experiences in Maes D and answered learners' questions. Most in-migrants are eager not only to learn the language but to imbibe the culture of their adopted country; this is the case for students from overseas as well as other parts of the UK.

The co-ordinating tutor for WfA at Bangor University, Elwyn Hughes, wrote in the Welsh magazine *Golwg* in 1989 that too much attention was sometimes paid by the media to learners from outside Wales. He viewed many of them as freaks, albeit *'freaks hoffus'* (likeable freaks) and stressed that more attention should be paid to *dysgwyr go iawn* (real learners), by which he meant those who are highly likely to stay in Wales. When Huw Lewis researched the learners at a residential WLPAN at Lampeter in 2001 he regarded some of the overseas learners as 'lone wolves' who did not really fall into any category. It is difficult to categorise motivations of students from overseas, particularly those with no family background in the language, who do not intend to settle in Wales. Pam Petro from the USA, who is half Hungarian and half German, has no Welsh connections. One cannot help asking the obvious '*Pam, Pam?*' (Why, Pam?) In response to friends' and relatives' questions about her reasons for studying Welsh at Harvard and spending a Summer vacation on an intensive Welsh course in Lampeter, Pam offered an explanation in her book *Travels in an Old Tongue*:

> I don't know. Maybe when I first went to Wales and unwittingly
> enrolled in an English department the old Welsh god of irony
> vowed to teach me a lesson and made me besotted with the place
> and its language (I made up the god of Irony but there really is an
> old Celtic god of panic, who comes in handy in cases of both
> travel and language study). To tell the truth, I really can't say why
> my desire to continue learning Welsh got so out of hand that I
> chose to pursue it on a five-month, fourteen-country crusade
> around the world. Perhaps I had a premonition of what Ursula
> Imadegawa would tell me in Tokyo. 'Pam,' she said 'You only
> regret what you *don't* do.'

Comments later in her book reveal more of the true motivation that
appeared to be linked with issues of community spirit and identity.
'Wales is still rural. I think it's a draw to the pastoral, to the sense of
community that you don't get in a city . . . '

Celebrities from a variety of walks of life have been amongst the
Welsh learners whose numbers have mushroomed during the latter
half of the twentieth and early twenty-first century. Within Wales,
famous Welsh learners include sportsmen Nigel Walker and Michael
Owen; sportswoman Tanni Grey-Thompson; the actors Ali Yassine
and Ruth Madoc, the news presenters Lucy Owen and Sara
Edwards; the weatherman Derek Brockway; the war veteran Simon
Weston, and surprisingly the acerbic journalist Janet Street-Porter.

Another surprising example is the English actress Stephanie
Cole, who has no Welsh roots, but learned Welsh in the 1970s, when
her aim was to appreciate the works of Dafydd ap Gwilym, whom she
regards as the Welsh Shakespeare. Another famous learner is the
astronaut, Dafydd Rhys Williams, born in Canada but with roots in
south Wales, who sent a Welsh-language message from outer space
in the 1990s.

Learners outside Wales
It is not easy to stay motivated to use Welsh outside Wales. Pamela
Petro uses spoken Welsh only very occasionally in the USA, and
Marilyn Lewis who learned Welsh in New Zealand in the 1980s
reports that appointment to a responsible lecturing post meant that

her Welsh studies could not continue. She now has no-one with whom to practise and her use of Welsh is limited to the occasional singing of Welsh hymns and visits to Wales.

Branches of CYD have been established overseas to enable learners to meet and use Welsh with fluent speakers. Many overseas learners of course, have no access to CYD. Craig Bohren laments that he no longer speaks Welsh in the United States despite gaining a high degree of fluency and giving the inaugural address at the opening of the Learners' tent at the 1978 National Eisteddfod. Had he settled in a large city such as Boston rather than in a thinly-populated rural area, he believes there would have been opportunities to maintain his fluency because of the greater availability of Welsh-speakers. In contrast, an example of an actively fluent learner overseas is Kevin Rottet, a linguist from Wisconsin, who learned so successfully that he was invited to teach Welsh on the Cwrs Madog, a week-long intensive Welsh course held annually at a variety of venues in the USA.

Chris Cope, from Minnesota, who learned through the BBC website, is another example of a highly-motivated learner in the USA. His efforts to teach himself have been so successful that Cardiff University offered him a place to study for a BA in Welsh in 2006. Chris stresses the importance of continuing to learn when reaching the inevitable plateaux common to all second-language learners, and the value of support from close family members. Dr Tim Jilg is another fluent learner from the USA who now works as a researcher in the Welsh Department at Cardiff University.

Learners, then, are studying Welsh for a variety of reasons. The strength and type of motivation may change as they learn. Some learners begin by only wanting a smattering, but become consumed by their interest in the language and culture, and progress to fluency. In the 1970s Margaret, a student in Cardiff, was eager to learn a practical skill, but was turned away as the class was full. She decided to give Welsh a try instead and was soon attending weekend and intensive courses. She now lives and works through the medium of Welsh in an area where Welsh is the language of the majority in the community. Others may begin intending to become fluent and soon decide they do not want to make the effort to do so, or may be hindered from doing so by life circumstances.

Learning a second language as an adult is quite an effort and involves a greater time commitment than many learners realise. Andrea, who has a higher degree and is well used to learning, commented in her journal, 'I thought it was going to be easy but it is not.' She attributed her preset ideas to advertisements for courses such as Linguaphone, which rarely refer to the fact that the student will have to expend considerable time and energy to learn a second language. Exaggerated claims by publishers, and titles such as *Welsh in Three Months* mean that learners become daunted early on when experience does not match up to expectations. Heini Gruffudd, a prominent figure in Welsh for Adults for over thirty years, and the author of many useful books for learners, believes that learners become disappointed as they expect fluency after an WLPAN course, or at least after a follow-up course. Heini is surely right in stressing that it is not attendance on courses of two or three hundred hours that produces fluency. This is the foundation on which learners must build. According to Heini, attendance on courses or exposure to the language for about one thousand five hundred hours is what produces confident speakers.

Susan Richardson, originally from Monmouthshire, who works as a writer and a creative writing tutor in Cardiff, expressed her struggles when learning, as well as her determination to succeed, in the poem used in the front of this book. As Susan studied French, German, Spanish, Italian and Latin at GCSE, and French and German at 'A' level, and continues to use all of these apart from Latin, it seems surprising that she found her efforts at learning Welsh so trying. However, time is a big issue for her, for as a writer she has to meet deadlines. Another issue for her is the difficulty of Welsh relative to other languages.

It is often suggested that Welsh is a particularly difficult language to learn, which is a self-perpetuating myth. Some Welsh-speakers may still have the mistaken notion that it is only possible for children to become fluent. It is not easy, however, to assess in absolute terms the difficulty of a particular language. An explanation of the widespread view that Welsh is particularly difficult is that most people in the UK have at some point dabbled in at least one European language at school even if they have nowhere near attained fluency. The Celtic languages have much less in common with

English than the Teutonic and Romance languages, despite the fact that Welsh has borrowed from English and Latin and has even preserved some lost English meanings.

Mark Abley sums up the situation: 'Although they (Welsh and English) belong to the vast Indo-European family, they perch on separate branches of the family tree.' To offset the differences, however, many learners have noted how much easier it is to learn to pronounce Welsh than it is for learners overseas to pronounce English, as Welsh is largely phonetic. Most of them also have higher motivation than they did in school, as adult students are learning of their own volition.

The struggle is only half over when the language has been mastered in class. Speaking skills must then be transferred to the community. If learners have used Welsh only in class and have not practised with first-language speakers, they will usually struggle to speak Welsh outside the safety of the classroom when the course ends. It's best to start *using* Welsh from day one.

Julie MacMillan won the Learner of the Year competition in 2007.

Listen to what Julie MacMillan, Learner of the Year 2007 says:

Learning a new language isn't easy but it is a lot of fun and you meet lots of wonderful, interesting people. I believe, to become fluent in a language all you need is a true desire to learn that language together with enthusiasm and determination. Three and a half years ago I started learning Welsh. I am a mother of two and worked part time. I asked the headmaster of my children's school if I could help in the school voluntarily, perhaps listening to the children read. That was the first serious step I took to become a fluent Welsh-speaker. From then on, I immersed myself in the Welsh Language every Thursday and Friday, as of course, no English is spoken at all, not even in the staff room. I believe I really threw myself in at the deep end and it was a sink or swim situation. I therefore found myself having to swim very hard!

I am a working mum, raising two children and was learning Welsh three times a week, while having to get up at 5.15 am three times a week and not returning home until 8.00 pm, where my children would be ready for bed and waiting for me to come home to give them a kiss *'nos da'* (goodnight). I truly believe if I could do it, with all the commitments I had, then there is hope for anyone, believe me!

Julie's Top Tips

- Do not worry about making mistakes, have a go and always laugh at your own mistakes
- Ymarfer, Ymarfer, Ymarfer! (Practise, Practise, Practise)
- Don't give up!
- Always remember: 'Gwell nag athro yw ymarfer' (Practice makes perfect)

Would you like to find out more?
Sandi Thomas, *You Don't Speak Welsh!* (Y Lolfa/Dinas, 2001)

Chapter 5
Dodging behind the shelves
– language switch

Learning it
> you're safe enough
> *but don't give up*
> the worst
> is still to come
> seven years in night class
> once a week wearing
> the teachers down
> your malice was all in the
> switch from classroom
> drills to breathless
> chattering on the
> Winter streets – *speaking*
> *it took courage.*

David Greenslade, 1992 (italics added)

David clearly had the necessary courage: he is now a fluent Welsh-speaker and writes in English and Welsh.

Making the in-laws suffer
Learning in class is one thing. Speaking Welsh outside is another, and learners have reported a variety of experiences when using the language in the community, some quite negative but others very positive. Those who persisted through the difficult times are glad they did so. Listen to Kim:

15 years ago I worked in the States ... One of my fellow-workers was a Japanese man with very little English. Another was an Italian woman who although her English was quite good, had an incredibly strong Italian accent and a peculiar way of saying English words. ... I can remember some tortured conversations with one or both of them, wishing just for some peace and quiet!

I can't help but think of these people sometimes when I'm speaking Welsh to people – I'm conscious that I may be making them suffer in the same way!

In her journal Kim then went on to ponder whether she was inflicting similar suffering on her in-laws:

In February I took the children on my own to my Welsh-speaking in-laws. I spoke mostly Welsh with them for about 2 hours. This is hard as I have known them for many years in English. It was morale boosting because, as a typical learner vs. West Walians, I have some good vocabulary which they comment on. My weakness is the fluidity that comes with using the right verbs in the right tenses. I can't quite put my finger on it but I always feel that Gordon's mother is relieved when I go back into English.

Practising a second language is not easy, as many students will bear witness. Zongren Liu from mainland China has written a fascinating account of his trials and successes when trying to practise English in the USA in *Two Years in the Melting Pot*. At first he resorted to using the television, even advertisements, to help him get to grips with day-to-day speech as he found the pace of modern life made it difficult to engage English speakers in casual conversation. Only when a young couple befriended him did he really benefit from regular practice. For both the learner and the first-language speaker it is not an easy situation and it is not difficult to understand that where there is a common language one or both parties will be tempted to fall back on it. Here's what Millie had to say:

E. is a retired teacher and member of *Merched y Wawr*. I met her in the shop and she always talks to me in Welsh very clearly and not fast and prompts gently. I am quite happy to meet her for this reason. I do not dodge behind the shelves.

There are times, however, when Millie and other learners have admitted to dodging first-language speakers. At a focus group in 2000 Kim let drop that she had sometimes crossed the street rather than face conversing in Welsh, and other members of the group admitted to the same reaction.

Not only learners dodge, however. As this chapter unfolds it will become clear that first-language speakers and even second-language speakers sometimes avoid using Welsh with learners.

Willingness to Communicate (WTC)

It was 'a truth universally acknowledged' that ability and aptitude made it easy for a second-language learner to become a fluent speaker. However, in recent years many scholars have stressed that students' willingness to communicate outside the classroom and regular practising of the language are key factors in a learner's success. Willingness to communicate (WTC) is becoming a buzz phrase among those interested in how adult language learners progress to fluency. Indeed many would argue that WTC, combined with strong motivation, is more important than ability. Christine Jones, who learned Welsh on the first ever WLPAN in Wales in 1973 and is now a Welsh for Adults tutor, told me she is convinced of this, as is Cathy who stressed at an AWLP focus group, 'Motivation is the key to success.'

Tanni Grey-Thompson, Britain's best-known paralympic athlete, believes this applies in all spheres, 'But at the highest level in any walk of life, natural talent is not enough ... You need the ability to push yourself as hard as you can, and need to be able to pick yourself up from disasters.'

However, many learners are subject to pressures that cause strong motivation to wane. Ideally, despite the inevitable plateaux and disappointing encounters with first-language speakers, the onus should be on an adult learner to persist. Many learners to date have been unable to do this. They have been daunted by the obstacles described in this book and cease learning, and using, Welsh altogether.

One of the main hindrances for learners who have attended Welsh classes for some time and have a good grounding in the language is lack of opportunity to use Welsh in the community. Many complain that it is difficult to persuade first-language speakers to hold a conversation in Welsh. Some are fearful of using it outside class and only aim to get by in understanding and reading the language. Others blame themselves for their lack of persistence outside class, describing disappointment and relief on returning to

English at the earliest opportunity. Mairi Higham wrote that in the early years of learning the switch to English arose not merely from the Welsh-speakers but also from her own ambivalence. Many learners feel exactly as Pamela Petro did when she was on the WLPAN in Lampeter, 'Every time one of us begins a sentence in English I wince under the twin reflexes of relief and shame.'

This is a complex issue and not one for which either first-language speakers or learners can be held responsible. Before we look at the learners' descriptions of the encouragement they have received outside class we will take a look at some of the negative comments.

'I hope no one will let him down'
In 1978 Craig Bohren commented in his speech in the Learners' Tent at the National Eisteddfod,

> *Rwy wedi cwrdd â chryn lawer oedd wedi dechrau ar gyrsiau Cymraeg gyda'r amcanion gorau yn y byd, oedd wedi dysgu hanfodion yr iaith yn dda, ond . . . dyma nhw'n uniaith Saesneg unwaith yn rhagor, Pam? . . . oherwydd nad oedd digon o gyfle iddyn nhw siarad Cymraeg yn gyson. Ac rwy'n sôn am siarad â Chymry Cymraeg. Peth hollol ddiwerth bron yw dysgwyr yn siarad â dysgwyr.* (I have met quite a few who have started on Welsh courses with the best intentions in the world, learned the essentials of the language well, but here they are monoglot English once again, Why? . . . because there was not enough opportunity for them to speak Welsh regularly. And I am talking about speaking with first-language Welsh-speakers. It is almost totally useless for learners to speak to learners.)

Many students have said that they prefer to practise with learners as they feel more relaxed, and such practice may be constructive up to a point. Sybil noted in her journal, 'Spoke quite a lot with the other learners in the house, much easier to speak with people at a similar level as they take as much time to think about things as I do, and don't use any unexpected words!'

However, as Craig states, in the long-term regular practice with first-language speakers is the best way forward.

Journals such as *Planet, Y Faner, Barn* and *Y Wawr* published accounts of learners' experiences in the 1970s and 1980s, several echoing Craig's view and reporting that the opportunity for practice generally was limited. J P Brown wrote in 1971 that, like many learners during this period, he experienced problems convincing Welsh-speakers that he could hold a conversation in Welsh. They would willingly exchange greetings and a simple comment on the weather, but they switched to English to communicate on other topics. He thought that 'the unwelcoming attitude was widespread and possibly typical'. In 1975 Cedric Maby wrote that at best he was regarded as an eccentric. On the whole he found shopkeepers more willing than farmers to converse with him and recalls as a young boy overhearing a shopkeeper saying to his mother, 'I hope no one will let him down.' Later he understood that she was concerned he would become disheartened if first-language speakers switched to English. Similarly Nicholas Jacobs wrote in 1974, 'In Wales the language for speaking to strangers is English', a practice he interpreted as a kind of courtesy. However, Nicholas believes a really committed learner will not be deterred from speaking Welsh.

In 1976 Geoffrey Turner wrote that a major problem for learners is the lack of opportunity to use the language in a bilingual society, even in the Welsh heartland areas:

Dyna un o broblemau'r dysgwyr, mi gredaf; eisiau siarad Cymraeg cymaint ag a ellir, a dyw hynny ddim yn hawdd bob amser mewn gwlad ddwyieithog, hyd yn oed mewn ardaloedd Cymraeg eu hiaith. Alla i ddim cofio pa mor aml rydw i wedi cael fy siomi yn fawr wrth fynd i mewn i dafarn mewn ardal Gymraeg a chlustfenio mewn anobaith i glywed yr hen iaith.

(This is one of the learners' problems, I believe; wanting to speak Welsh as much as they can and this is not always easy in a bilingual country, even in Welsh-speaking areas. I cannot remember how often I have been very disappointed by going into a pub in a Welsh-speaking area and eavesdropping with no hope of hearing the old language.)

A particularly negative view of learners and first-language speakers appeared under the pseudonym Gregory in a letter to *Safiad*, a publication which dealt with Welsh-language issues in the late 1980s:

I don't think these Welsh ******* are serious about preserving their language. As I've told you before they moan a lot about us English moving in to the place and not learning the things etc. but you should listen to some of them taking the **** out of the Anglo-Saxons who take the trouble to contort their mouths into impossible shapes in order to pronounce Welsh words. Some of these learners or 'discoves' as they're called come to the pub to put theory to practice every Wednesday night and a ****** motley bunch they are too. Misguided in the extreme in my opinion. But here's the funny thing – the local Welshies won't go near 'em! And if one of the 'discoves' happen to corner a Taff a look of blind panic comes into his eyes and he immediately looks for the quickest escape route. Furthermore the misguided Englishman will be speaking Welsh and the Taff will insist on answering in English!

Gregory's observation that *Cymry Cymraeg* are diffident about speaking to learners and may even avoid doing so corroborates from a very different perspective other evidence of this trend.

By the 1990s when learners were no longer such a rare species reports continued of learners who often struggled to find first-language speakers willing to provide much needed practice opportunities. Noragh Jones described the following reaction from an English person living in rural Wales, who explained why he did not make the effort to learn Welsh:

. . . especially when I recall the misfortunes of some of my colleagues who have tried and been defeated by the unwillingness of the Welsh-speaking co-workers to speak Welsh to them. I distinctly remember poor old Jonathan hunting down the Welsh-speakers in the coffee room, and having to nail them to the wall to get them to speak to him. He ultimately succeeded, partly because he was a Methodist lay preacher, I suspect, but also because he was an obstinate northerner, not easily discouraged. Whereas I'm a sort of Londoner, though of course I wouldn't want to live there now, I'll settle for around here – so long as I don't have to learn the language.

The poet Ifor ap Glyn, who worked for a while as a tutor in Cardiff University's Centre for Teaching Welsh to Adults, wrote about this in a poem in 1999:

> *... ond wnân nhw ddim siarad â dysgwyr.*
> *Rhyfedd yntê?*
> (... and they won't speak to learners.
> Strange isn't it?)

In 1993 Pamela Petro described her experiences on an WLPAN in Lampeter in the New York Times. Her main problem was finding suitable practice opportunities:

> I did find some residents who would indulge me ... but most people felt they were doing me a favor by speaking English. About six weeks into the course I began to entertain a desire to speak Welsh beyond the Porter Cabin (*sic*). I'd stride into the *Swyddfa'r Post* (Post Office), or a bakery where a knot of townspeople would be speaking in Welsh; invariably the attendant would look me cheerfully in the eye and ask, 'And what'll be today, dear?' This wasn't a put-down; it was simply the problem inherent in learning a lesser-used language. In Wales everyone speaks English, so when it's your turn and you're at the head of a long line, it's hard not to communicate in the first-language that comes to mind ...

Even today there are many reports of learners who have been disappointed when first-language speakers turn to English. Here's how two advanced AWLP students felt: 'Sometimes people do not wait until I have found the word. They try to help me – they turn to English – aargh!'

And, 'You put yourself on the line, there's no shield, if they reject you on language you're rejected, not really taken seriously, condescended to. As if they're saying, "Speak English, it's much nicer for both of us." It's demoralising and I wonder why do I bother?'

It is often the more advanced learners who are most distressed by first-language speakers switching to English. When students are close to fluency, they may feel the first-language speaker is making a judgment not only about their linguistic skills but also about their

Gwen Awbery, a mother-tongue Welsh-speaker, has had interesting experiences with other Welsh-speakers switching to English.

acceptance within the local Welsh-speaking community.

Even in the traditional heartland areas of north and west Wales, where there is more opportunity to use the language in daily life, some learners have found that first-language speakers switch to English. Alison Layland, for instance, who lives in such an area, has experienced difficulties in persuading some local people to use Welsh with her for day-to-day activities – despite her success in winning several prizes for her Welsh skills and publishing stories and articles in Welsh-language journals.

Gwen Awbery, a mother-tongue speaker, and co-ordinating lecturer in Welsh for Adults until 2008, commented that this may not be because they are learners. Despite her obvious fluency, she has noticed that when she visits west Wales shopkeepers and other business people address her in English, and it takes some time and persistence on her part for them to switch to Welsh with her. It could well be that inhabitants of the traditional heartland areas are just not used to speaking Welsh to those who sound as if they are from outside their area, and automatically turn to English. Gwen does not believe that the switch to English with learners is necessarily linked with a low standard of the learners' Welsh.

Other AWLP students reported that Welsh-speakers turn to English with the learners at Welsh-medium nurseries and mother and toddler groups, where learners and Welsh-speakers are inclined to form separate groups. Lydia reported:

At *Ti a Fi* (Mother & Toddler) you tend to get two main groups, one of which is made up of Welsh learners and the other of first-language Welsh-speakers and, although I do try and interact with both groups, my ability to converse with first-language speakers is limited and they do not seem very good at accommodating me.

In fact, quite surprisingly, they seem happier to speak to me in English than Welsh (unless this has something to do with my pained expression).

And Sharon said:

It was my turn to be the parent on duty at *Ysgol Feithrin* (Nursery School). I asked the leader not to translate into English for me as my understanding is better than my spontaneous conversation, but she kept forgetting, which was frustrating because I began to feel a bit alienated and could not summon up enough confidence to speak Welsh to her.

When I visited Welsh-medium nurseries and mother and toddler groups it became clear to me why learners were disappointed, as I could see that it was difficult for them to persuade first-language speakers to maintain conversations in Welsh. Surprisingly in one group the leader, a second-language learner, who had kept translating for Sharon, hardly used Welsh with the learners, and even offered them drinks in English. As the students were intermediate and advanced level this was quite disappointing.

Miquel Strubell de Trueta points out that language-learning is a lifelong experience, even in our first language!

Language switch is not something that happens only in Wales, of course. It takes place with Gaelic learners in Scotland and Ireland, and farther afield where there is a language of wider communication. There is such an emphasis on learning English in China that learners of Chinese have difficulty finding an educated person who is content to talk only in Chinese. I have experienced this trend first hand. In 2000 I tried to practise German in Germany, and despite quite a high degree of fluency found that many Germans who could speak English would switch to English in order to practise their English-speaking skills! In Catalonia learners have reported that first-language speakers often switch to Spanish when there is anxiety or hesitation on the learner's part. Here are some tips for Welsh learners from Miquel Strubell de Trueta, a lecturer in the Department of Languages and Cultures at the Open University of Catalonia.

Miquel's Top Tips for Welsh Learners

- When you try and practise your Welsh outside the classroom, bear in mind many Welsh-speakers will switch to English quite automatically. Just carry on regardless, in Welsh! It happens the whole time in Catalonia (with Catalan-speakers switching to Spanish quite unconsciously) and adult learners complain bitterly about this.
- Try and plan your use of Welsh, as you start to get a grasp of it. Say short phrases or sentences to people, that you can rehearse beforehand.
- Start using Welsh in relaxing situations: to speak to little children, for instance, or to other learners outside the classroom.
- Make an effort to remember how much less you could speak just a few months ago: this will keep your spirits up! Language learning is a lifelong experience, even in our first language.
- Even opera singers drink their little glass of sherry before going on stage in the first act: so a little Dutch courage will loosen your tongue no end (provided you don't have to drive later!).
- Think up a good response (in English!) well before anyone ever dares demean your early efforts to speak Welsh. Having the answer up your sleeve will give you more social confidence.

Language switch is happening all over the world and it takes a strong will to resist the temptation to lapse back into the common language, in our case, English. However, the rewards are great for those who persist, as many learners who are now fluent in Welsh, will testify. Tim Jilg is a particularly good example of this. He began learning in Ohio where he had a Welsh-speaking friend who always spoke to Tim in English. Tim persisted in speaking Welsh and after nine months his friend responded in Welsh.

Tim's top tips

- Refuse to speak English
- If you do not understand vocabulary – ask!
- Read aloud when you are learning alone

Eventually Tim was fortunate enough to be able to immerse himself in Welsh by sharing a house in Cardiff with three other first-language Welsh-speakers. Three months later he was fluent. Tim also worked very hard, as when he attended the WLPAN for three hours a day he was also spending three hours studying, as well as listening to *Radio Cymru* and watching *S4C*.

It takes a great deal of will-power to do what Jonathan Langfield, a learner from Gloucester, does. Jonathan pretends he is in a foreign country where English is not spoken. It works, though, as Jonathan has only been learning for just over a year and is able to make conversation in Welsh with first-language speakers. He does have an ideal immersion opportunity,

Even though Jonathan Langfield hails from Gloucester, he speaks Welsh with his Welsh-speaking wife and every Welsh-speaker he encounters.

though, as he has married a first-language Welsh-speaker.

Jonathan's top tips

- Pretend English is not available
- Do not worry about mistakes

Of course, the immersion opportunities Tim and Jonathan had are not available to all. However, everyone can insist on speaking Welsh to all the Welsh-speakers they know even if they respond in English.

Cyngor tu hwnt i'm gobaith (Advice far beyond my hopes)

Many learners are delighted with the help and support they have received from first-language speakers. John Gillibrand, Learner of the Year 1990, paid tribute to the people of Dolgellau who struggled to teach him Welsh, and Sue Massey, Learner of the Year in 2005, commented:

> I was born and raised in Ellesmere Port and I didn't have the first idea how to speak Welsh until I joined the WLPAN course in Bangor. I'm lucky that I've been able to practise my Welsh so often with friends in the band. Practising makes such a difference.

Membership of a group such as a band or a choir where there is regular contact with Welsh-speakers makes a big difference to a learner's practice opportunities. Similarly belonging to a society such as *Merched y Wawr* helps learners' confidence develop. Noragh Jones believes she would never have spoken Welsh but for the support of local Welsh-speakers, especially the *Merched y Wawr*:

> They welcomed me to their meetings, even though for the first year I used to sit like a mouse, afraid to try out my Welsh among such experts. But I listened and finally I was able to understand what they were going on about, and then I did speak out, and they all turned round and looked at me, as if the cat had started to talk! . . . Without these women I would never have been able to do what I had to do – settle in the village, and improve my Welsh to the point where I could get a professional bilingual post, and make good friends.

Lynne Evans praises Welsh-speakers in West Wales. She appealed for help from a Welsh-speaker when her efforts at learning through books, the Bible, and radio only met with limited success, '*Cefais ganddi groeso, cefnogaeth a chyngor y tu hwnt i'm gobaith.*' (I received welcome, support and advice from her far beyond my hopes.)

In a similar vein, Lois Martin-Short praised first-language Welsh-speakers who came to help learners at CYD realising that it was not always easy for them,

> *Mae'n waith caled i ni siarad ond rydw i'n gwybod nad yw hi'n hawdd i wrando ar ddysgwyr ac i feddwl am ffyrdd syml i drafod pethau.*
> (Speaking is hard work for us but I know that it isn't easy to listen to learners and think of a simple way to discuss things.)

Lois also praised a friend on whom she could rely to speak Welsh consistently and who would turn to simple Welsh rather than English when necessary.

While R S Thomas was greatly helped by Rev H D Owen and his wife in Manafon in the 1940s, he was aware that he was taking up their time and energy:

> Almost every week through all weathers he would walk to the home of HD having done his homework ... He was given a warm welcome by HD and his wife, Megan in their home, and after struggling on for years at their expense he came to speak Welsh quite satisfactorily, although it took a long time, as he did not wish to impose on these kind people too often.

Diane Cooney wrote of her gratitude for the support she received from Welsh-speakers but admitted that it was hard work to understand them initially; determination and perseverance were vital. When Rosemary Jones moved from London to Cellifor, a small village in north-east Wales, the support of local first-language speakers allowed her to become sufficiently proficient to teach technology through the medium of Welsh, '*O'r cychwyn cefais gymorth gwerth chweil gan fy nghymdogion a mamau'r ysgol Feithrin.*' (From the beginning I received worthwhile help from neighbours and the mothers at the nursery school.)

It seems that when Welsh-speakers are assigned a specific task they rise to the occasion. This was certainly the case for clergyman Patrick Thomas who, when working in a Welsh heartland area, was supported and helped by his parishioners, who immersed him 'in a sea of Welsh'. Patrick's parishioners had been asked to do so by the rector and so the ambivalent attitude to using Welsh with learners disappeared as the first-language speakers tried to fulfil a stipulated task. Interestingly Janet Ryder AM praised many local people who helped her when she was learning, but finds that now she is a confident speaker they tend to speak English to her!

Some AWLP students noted successful conversations with first-language speakers in their journals, as did Lydia:

> This afternoon I took Emyr to *Ti a Fi*. I tried to speak as much Welsh to him as possible. One of the Welsh-speaking grandmothers came over and chatted a little bit to me. I tried to speak Welsh back and she said that she would always try to speak to me in Welsh so that I can practise.

Sybil was positive about the help she had received, but like Lois Martin-Short realised that it could be hard work for first-language speakers to listen to learners:

'Use it or lose it!' says Steve Morris about speaking Welsh.

Fluent speakers tend to use parts of the language that I don't know as it comes so easily to them, making conversation difficult. Everyone I have spoken to has been helpful and encouraging, but I do find it embarrassing when my part of the conversation takes so long, and I have to ask people to repeat things.

Here are some tips for *dysgwyr* from Steve Morris, a lecturer at Swansea University, an experienced WfA tutor and researcher, on how learners can transfer their classroom Welsh to the community.

Steve's Tips
From the classroom to the community

- Try to use Welsh wherever you can and with whoever you can as soon as possible. If you live in a Welsh-speaking community, use Welsh first with everyone you meet. Don't worry if they answer you in English! Keep going!/*Daliwch ati*! Remember, it is normal to use Welsh in these communities so you're not doing anything different to the norm.

- Find out where the local Menter Iaith is and make sure you are kept aware of all the activities organised in your area and go to them (with a friend!); if you have children in a Welsh medium school, offer to help with reading in school or Parent Teacher Association (PTA) activities.

- If you live in a community where Welsh is not the every day language, look for other ways to use the language: you'll be surprised how many Welsh-speakers there are out there! Try to find a neighbour or work colleague who knows the language; look for the orange 'iaith gwaith' logo which shows you who speaks Welsh in shops, businesses etc.

- And finally . . . and most importantly: Use it or Lose it! Sometimes you will have to persevere and even be stubborn – as nearly all Welsh-speakers are bilingual, reverting to English can be the easier option for some. Don't forget, though, that once you've done that, it is then even more difficult to change back and establish a relationship with someone through the medium of Welsh. It's much better to keep going in Welsh – after all, we all have a choice and you are just exercising yours to use Welsh rather than English.

Would you like to find out more?
Lynda Pritchard Newcombe, *Social Context and Fluency in L2 Learners* (Multilingual Matters, 2007)
Pamela Petro, *Travels in an Old Tongue* (Harper Collins, 1997)
Tanni Grey-Thompson, *Aim High* (Accent Press, 2007)

Chapter 6
'I'm terrified of learners!'
Why do first-language speakers switch?

Medi James, an experienced Welsh for Adults tutor, wrote in *Y Faner Newydd* in 1998:

> *Does dim prinder siaradwyr Cymraeg ond mae prinder defnyddwyr y Gymraeg. Lleisiau ar y ffôn yn llawer rhy barod i droi i'r Saesneg, cydweithwyr mewn swyddfeydd yn rhy brysur, a gweithwyr siopau'n rhy anwybodus i sylweddoli'r trysor sy ganddyn nhw heb ei ddefnyddio – ddim yn cynnig cyfle i'w cwsmeriaid ofyn am dorth o fara neu bwys o datws yn y Gymraeg. Pan feddyliwch chi am y myrdd o amgylchiadau dibwys, ddydd ar ôl dydd i ddefnyddio iaith syml i roi cyfle i'r dysgwyr yma. Ymadroddion syml rydyn ni'n eu hail-adrodd dro ar ôl tro mewn bywyd bob dydd. Mewn sefyllfaoedd dyddiol fel hyn mae perthynas yn cael ei greu a'i feithrin ac o hyn daw hyder a boddhad i'r dysgwr a'r Cymro.*

(There is no shortage of Welsh-speakers but there is a shortage of Welsh users. Voices on the phone too ready to turn to English, colleagues in offices too busy, shop workers unaware of the treasure at their disposal, if only to offer customers the opportunity to ask for a loaf of bread or a pound of potatoes in Welsh. When you think of the myriad of insignificant circumstances, day after day where simple language could be used to give a chance to these learners. Simple phrases that we repeat over and over daily. In everyday situations like this a relationship is created and nurtured and from this comes the confidence and satisfaction for the learner and the first-language Welsh-speaker.)

Scared of 'posh' learners!

According to Avril, a first-language Welsh-speaker who works in Cardiff, '*Bydd newid meddylfryd siaradwyr Cymraeg yn dalcen caled.*' (It will be a difficult challenge to change the mindset of Welsh-speakers towards learners.) Why?

There are numerous reasons for some first-language speakers' unwillingness to converse in Welsh to learners. One difficulty which I think is highly significant is the Cymry Cymraeg's lack of confidence in their own language skills. Heini Gruffudd commented in *Barn* in 1979 that many first-language speakers who attended English-medium schools and had not received formal Welsh lessons may panic and feel inferior when they hear learners using words unfamiliar to them. Over the years many experienced tutors such as Llinos Dafis have made the same observation and many learners have observed this.

The American anthropologist Carol Trosset, who learned Welsh on an WLPAN in Lampeter, and the writers Noragh Jones and Pamela Petro, view Welsh-speakers' reticence as a symptom of lack of confidence in their ability to speak their own language accurately Similarly, Jane Hafren Beynon, one of the runners up in the Learner of the Year competition in 2004, has heard time and again in Cwm Gwendraeth, where she tries to encourage liaison between learners and Welsh-speakers,*'Dydy fy Nghymraeg i ddim yn ddigon da i ddysgwyr.'* (My Welsh isn't good enough for learners.)

At the 2008 National Eisteddfod in Cardiff, Ann, a first-language speaker from Bangor, described a learner she knew who spoke better Welsh than first-language speakers. When I enquired further she said her grammar was perfect and she had a very wide vocabulary, often using words that locals did not know. Another interviewee at the Eisteddfod, Beti, originally from west Wales, said that she spoke to learners at a rambling club but she wished she had a wider vocabulary so that she could be of more help.

Again, this is not a problem unique to Wales. As far afield as Indonesia, for instance, the linguist, Peggy Dufon had problems persuading first-language speakers to use Javanese when she was learning. They always switched to Indonesian, behaviour she attributes in part to the fact that many Javanese are afraid to make mistakes.

Welsh-speakers' views that the learner's Welsh is in some way better than their own are commonplace. Some first-language speakers told Kathleen Greenwood her Welsh was *'rhy berffaith'* (too perfect), Noragh Jones' Welsh was described as 'too good', Carol Trosset was made aware that her Welsh was 'too correct', and

Pamela Petro was told she spoke 'posh Welsh'. West-Walians declared that Mairi Higham's Welsh was 'more educated' than that of first-language speakers. Noragh Jones recorded:

> 'Poor man', said a church warden in the Tregaron area to me, 'our last vicar – he learnt Welsh, for we have bilingual services in our church, and he was a conscientious young man. But it was a pity he learnt it so well. He spoke such a pure form of Welsh that nobody around here knew what he was talking about . . . '

Kathryn Jones when researching learners in north-east Wales in 2000 reported on learners who had been described as 'more accurate' than first-language speakers. Similarly students interviewed for a research project by Haydn Hughes in 2003 volunteered, '*Rhai o bobl yn dweud bod geiriau fi – fel dysgwr – yn well na eiriau nhw.*' (Some people say that my words – as a learner – are better than their words.)

One of Millie's Welsh-speaking contacts commented when Millie bemoaned that she did not practise with her, 'I never speak to learners. I'm terrified of them.' When asked why, she responded that their vocabulary was far greater than her own.

Sometimes learners are aware of first-language speakers' lack of confidence. Several interviewees in a study by the Welsh Consumer Council (WCC) in 2005 reported that Welsh-speakers sometimes seemed hesitant to talk to them as they viewed the learners as speaking 'proper' Welsh with an understanding of correct grammar and vocabulary. One student commented, 'When you speak to some Welsh-speakers they don't like speaking to learners. They are almost frightened that I might have a better standard of Welsh than them.'

Similar observations appeared in learners' journals. Kim, for instance, was surprised that her parents-in-law lacked confidence in their Welsh skills, '*Maen nhw'n dweud fy mod i'n siarad yn 'posh' gyda mwy o geiriau cywir na nhw!*' (They say that I speak 'posh' with more correct words than they do!)

And Cathy thought that when Welsh-speaking parents from school remarked, 'It's much easier to be your friend in English,' they were commenting on their own Welsh not on hers.

Rachel noted:

At Llanishen Leisure Centre – at a children's birthday party! – I spoke to two friends who are both Welsh-speaking to arrange a mothers' night out in Cardiff and a shopping trip to Cardiff. One of the mothers (Nansi) always talks to me in Welsh, her parents are English-speaking and sent her to a Welsh school in Pontypridd. The other mother (Sandra) only speaks to me in Welsh if Nansi is there too as I think she feels that her Welsh isn't "proper" Welsh, it's much more colloquial/west Walian Welsh as she is from Llanelli.

When Huw Lewis studied learners in west Wales in 2001 he found many first-language speakers were anxious about speaking to those who use scholarly language rather then the local dialect. On his return to west Wales after years abroad, he had attempted to use more erudite Welsh than he had used earlier in the local community and several people he spoke to for the first time formed the impression he had learned Welsh. The anthropologist Fiona Bowie also found that only the more educated were willing to speak Welsh to her in north-west Wales, the less educated preferring to speak English.

Interestingly when the novelist Siân James translated her book *Small Country* into Welsh, she was careful to use the vocabulary that local people normally used in day-to-day conversation on the street. In a radio interview on *Radio Cymru* she said that she avoided words such as '*yr orsaf*' for the station as only teachers and learners would use such words and locals would say '*stasiwn*'. Perhaps it is not merely first-language speakers' lack of confidence in their own skills but a general feeling of awkwardness as the learners' vocabulary sounds unnatural and grates on the Cymry Cymraeg. Jean Preston recalls asking the way to the *meddygfa* in her early days in living in mid-Wales and the locals taking some time to realise that she was asking directions to '*y syrjeri*'. This issue is summed up neatly by Alison Layland:

Dydi'r Cymry Cymraeg ddim yn iwsio'r un geiriau ag y mae dysgwyr yn eu defnyddio! Enghraifft arall mae pawb yn dweud practiso nid ymarfer y rhan fwyaf o'r amser yn ein pentre ni.

(The Welsh-speakers do not use the same words as the learners. Another example – in our village everyone uses *practiso* and not *ymarfer* most of the time.)

Welsh-speakers, particularly those with no educational background in Welsh, often count and give dates in English. An English neighbour once asked my cousin in Ludlow whether numbers and dates existed in the Welsh language, because when passively listening to *Radio Cymru* she often heard Welsh conversations in which dates and numbers in English were interspersed. This happens in other countries where languages live side by side. In Malta, for example, conversations in Maltese are spattered with English numbers and dates. Such tendencies do not inspire learners, sometimes bolstering the notion that languages such as Welsh and Maltese are less suitable for use in the commercial world than English. However, it is easy to understand how the situation has arisen if the Welsh or Maltese speaker has been educated through the medium of English, and Welsh or Maltese is *iaith yr aelwyd* (the language of the hearth).

An insignificant language?
Welsh-speakers' diffidence about their language skills may also be linked with the negative attitudes that speakers of lesser-used languages often hold about their mother tongue. In Wales there has been a tendency to view Welsh as inferior to English, a phenomenon rooted in history. A particular contributor to this was the impact of the HM Commissioners' report of inquiry into the state of education in Wales in 1847, known generally as *Brad y Llyfrau Gleision* (Treachery of the Blue Books), which attributed most educational, social, economic and cultural disadvantages to the maintenance of the Welsh language. The long-term effects of this report were still in evidence in the twentieth century, and produced in many Welsh leaders a desire to make themselves as Anglicised as possible. Nevertheless, in others such as Emrys ap Iwan, M D Jones and O M Edwards, the evidence of English contempt inspired action to promote the language.

The Welsh have never been good at promoting themselves and their culture on the world stage. It has been a feature of Welsh culture, for example, particularly in past generations, not 'to show off' or 'put yourself forward'. In the USA, where the kilt and the shamrock are generally known to be linked with Scotland and Ireland, the Welsh icons such as the red dragon and the leek do not benefit to such a degree from what market researchers call 'brand recognition'. I have received mail from the USA to 'Cardiff, England', but I doubt whether inhabitants of Edinburgh or Dublin have received mail addressed to 'Edinburgh, England' or 'Dublin, England'. High profile Welsh-speaking celebrities such as the opera singer Bryn Terfel and the singer and presenter Aled Jones, who have gained world-wide fame, are helping to bring about a gradual change, and Wales is becoming more confident about the value of her language and culture.

Although Wales is becoming more optimistic about her place in the world and the value of her language, long-held attitudes may be resistant to change. Learners, particularly those from outside Wales, still report that first-language speakers are surprised in their interest in a tongue as 'insignificant' as Welsh. While first-language speakers might understand an individual's desire to learn some greetings, many cannot conceive of anyone, particularly those from outside Wales, aiming for fluency. The situation is complicated by the generally negative attitude to fluency in a second language in the UK. In 1979 Heini Gruffudd wrote in *Barn* about the experiences of Padrig, a Welsh learner from Brittany, who contrasted the attitude of the British, who rarely expect to learn other languages, with that of the continentals, who are used to speaking several languages. While it is common world-wide for individuals today to speak more than one language, and there are more bilingual people in the world than monolingual, becoming fluent in a second language in the UK is not usually seen as the norm but a special achievement.

'We knew them first in English'
On other occasions, reluctance to speak in Welsh on the first-language speaker's part is associated with the difficulty of changing from English to Welsh in the case of a friend or family member who has previously used English. Jill Roberts, when learning in Aberystwyth, found that her friends who had known her as an English speaker could only exchange pleasantries before lapsing into English. This was the experience of several AWLP students. Listen to

Alan: 'Huw and family came this morning. We mostly speak English, which disappoints me, but when you have a long friendship with someone it is difficult to relax and converse in a language you have only been learning for four years and you are in your forties!'

Problems of this kind are usually intensified when dealing with members of the family. For instance when I interviewed Mervyn, mainly through the medium of Welsh at the National Eisteddfod, he said that he uses Welsh regularly outside the home but rarely with his family, even though communicating with his wife and children was his initial motivation for learning: *'Dim ond fi a'r gath oedd ddim yn siarad Cymraeg yn ein tŷ ni.'* (Only the cat and I did not speak Welsh in our house.)

Similarly, Roger Fenton reported there were many bungled attempts before he eventually succeeded in conversing with his wife in Welsh on a regular basis, although for some time previously he had been conversing confidently with many first-language speakers in west Wales. And despite her fluency, Mairi Higham's in-laws in Cardiff always speak English to her as this is what they spoke when they first knew her. The only member of the family who uses Welsh with her is Sioned Glyn, her sister-in-law who lives in an area of north Wales where Welsh is still widely used on a day-to-day basis. Sioned commented, 'I have always spoken Welsh to Mairi from the very beginning, but when I am in Cardiff I find it very strange because all my family turn to English.'

As friends and family are such a valuable resource for practising it might help if tutors set homework for learners to interview or discuss specific topics with family members.It might also help if learners developed a strategy of practising for a few minutes each day with someone close to them. They can then gradually build this up, until it becomes natural to speak Welsh together as the learner gains fluency. The formality of this arrangement, and the psychological aspect of 'helping with homework' might also help the first-language Welsh-speakers, giving them a structure of 'language practice'. They would also see the learner improving week by week, which would encourage both parties, and it is likely that more Welsh conversation would evolve.

Not with my parents!

Some learners say their children enjoy helping them with Welsh. However, some children can be particularly unhelpful and exacerbate learners' hesitancy:

> My children go to Welsh medium primary school and are regarded by my first-language Welsh-speaking neighbours as being indistinguishable from first-language Welsh-speakers. However, they (my children) find my attempts at speaking Welsh excruciatingly amusing but refuse to explain where I am going wrong. Conversations therefore last a few minutes only before they collapse into English. With my exam coming up I have been promised more co-operation – we shall see. I suspect that they like having a language in which they can talk and which they think I cannot understand.

Rees has two teenage children who attend Welsh school, but they were not mentioned in his journal. At an interview, however, Rees said his sons never used Welsh at home, and it would be impossible to practise with them as every time they hear their parents using any Welsh they laugh. They are only overheard using Welsh at home when mimicking teachers.

Penny Wingfield from Aberconwy wrote in *Y Wawr*:

> *Rŵan mae Russell yn dysgu Cymraeg yn yr ysgol a mae o'n ei defnyddio efo plant eraill, ond fel arfer dydy o ddim isio siarad efo fi. Dwi'n nabod teuluoedd eraill efo'r un broblem ond mae gyda ni obaith y bydd pethau'n well pam mae'r plant yn tyfu. Maen nhw'n gwybod bod gyda ni ddiddordeb yn yr iaith.*
>
> (Now Russell is learning Welsh in school and he is using it with other children but usually he doesn't want to speak to me. I know other families with the same problem but we are hopeful that things will change when the children grow. They know that we are interested in the language.)

At a focus group all learners agreed with Cathy's comment, 'If you're very motivated you won't be too bothered about your family's response'. Cathy rightly lays great store by motivation, as the key to overcoming so many hindrances to using a second language. However, lack of support from family members, who are a ready-made practice opportunity, may cause even the strongest motivation to fade.

Tiredness
Learners and tutors are aware that speaking a new language can bring on discouragement and fatigue. However, there is little awareness of first-language speaker weariness when trying to help learners. When Derek, a learner of German, Russian and Finnish, was interviewed by the world expert on language learning, Earl Stevick, he stressed that this may well be the case particularly if it is difficult for the first-language speaker to follow the learner's accent:

> As you go from one language to another, the sheer exhaustion that follows the first time you use the language in a social evening is hard to describe! And it works in the other direction also. I think we leave the first-language speakers as worn out as we are

Pronunciation and Accent – big issues
Patrick Thomas, now a fluent second-language speaker, is aware that *dysgwyr* often complain how difficult it is to persuade Welsh-speakers to talk to them in Welsh. He attributes their reluctance to several factors: a fear of seeming impolite; concern that either the learner or the Welsh-speaker may be misunderstood; the awkwardness of switching to Welsh when a relationship has already been established in English. He also stresses that Welsh spoken with a non-Welsh accent can grate painfully on some Welsh-speakers' ears.

A study by Maria Aguado Ball in 1998 showed a link between learners' accents and the willingness of first-language speakers to use Welsh with them. Six out of seven specialists interviewed by Haydn Hughes in 2003 also made a connection between the learners' accent and language switch. According to one, Elwyn Hughes, first-language speakers in north Wales were willing to speak Welsh with learners from south Wales with a Welsh accent and intonation, but spoke English to those who spoke Welsh with an English accent. He believes that extrovert learners who are willing to imitate Welsh intonation are more likely to be accepted by Welsh-speakers than those who speak accurately but have an unfamiliar accent. Elwyn stressed that while first-language speakers will easily forgive learners for making grammatical and syntactic errors, they find a poor accent very difficult to tolerate.

This is something Pat Metcalfe has learned:

A dw i wedi dysgu, sdim ots os wyt ti'n gwneud camgymeriadau – y peth yw i ddal at i, beth bynnag – sdim y gramadeg sy'n or-bwysig, ond i gadw ati – ac yn SWNIO yn iawn. Mae clust dynwared 'da fi – wi'n lwcus. Rydw i'n gallu swnio fel 'un ohonon ni' fel dwedodd un o'r cymdogion, unwaith. Lyfli.

(I have learned that it doesn't matter if you make mistakes – the thing is to stick at it anyway – it's not the grammar that's important but sticking at it – and to SOUND good. I have a mimic's ear – I'm lucky. I can *sound* like 'one of us' as one of the neighbours said once. Lovely.)

Derek, Earl Stevick's interviewee concurs:

When I am learning a new language, I try to have just as little foreign accent as possible. . . . I have found in dealing with foreigners that their knowledge of grammar and vocabulary didn't make a big difference. The heavier their accent the less they were understood. So I have concluded that for me, learning pronunciation is just as important as learning grammar, if not more so.

Competent learners often still struggle with pronunciation and strive for a more realistic Welsh accent. 'R' may be a troublesome letter for those from outside Wales who are not accustomed to so much 'r' rolling. When even first-language speakers such as the eminent poet, Menna Elfyn, describe struggling with 'r' as a young person, we should not be surprised that those from outside Wales are grappling with it:

Heb nerth yn fy ngheg,
Dysgais redeg yr yrfa yn stond,
Heb rychwantu'r nendwr;
Heb y llythyren fawr, mewn llyffethair own,
Rhyw greadur mewn magl yn ei gwendid,
Yn nadu, heb im dafod chwaith i rwydo'r byd,
Cael fy rhaffo gan eraill a wnawn
– i dras y bras a'r bregus.
Beius ar wefus wrth honcian cytseiniaid,
Methu rhedeg reiat na throi campau'n rhempus.

Weak in the mouth,
I learned to run, treading air, the yr race
avoiding rolls in the roof, and side-stepping
the big letter; in fetters, I was
a creature snared in its own weakness,
whimpering without a tongue to net the world,
roped and branded by others,
consigned to the brood of rickety and rough,
gone in the mouth, a honker of consonants,
barred from running riot or feats of derring-do.

Menna Elfyn (2001)

The letters 'll' and 'ch' may also be troublesome for learners, particularly for those from outside Wales. Interestingly Abdul-Aziz Barazi from Syria, who is learning in north Wales has said that his knowledge of Arabic has been a great help to him when pronouncing such letters, and that he has far fewer problems with pronunciation than do monoglot English-speakers.

Rhythm

Jonathan Harnum, in his book *How to Blow Your Own Horn*, explains that 'Rhythm is the essential glue that binds music together. Rhythm is so important that without it music wouldn't exist.' The right rhythm is essential for language learners too, and in Welsh the right *goslef* (intonation) is very important to first-language speakers, though many of them may be unaware of it. The stress in Welsh usually falls on the penultimate (i.e. the last but one) syllable. There are some exceptions such as plurals ending in 'eydd' e.g. *amgueddfeydd* (museums) where it falls at the end and some words ending in 'au' where it also falls at the end e.g. *glanhau* (to clean). This is an area where learners can benefit by listening carefully to Welsh-speakers' intonation, and imitating it – particularly useful when a learner wishes to sound like the Welsh-speakers in his or her particular community.

Another of Earl Stevick's interviewees, Daoudi, came to realize this:

> I learned Farsi in Iran. In my early attempts to get the pronunciation, I was making (or at least thought I was making) the same sounds as they were, but I was totally incomprehensible to them. Then I decided to use my ears to pick up the rhythm of their language. Once I started speaking Farsi in their rhythm, I was comprehensible to them even though sometimes my vowels and consonants were a little different from theirs.

> I also found that though my Farsi vocabulary was not very extensive, my speech appeared to be more acceptable to them than the speech of several other people from my part of the world. This was true even though those other people had better vocabularies than I did.

Something must be done!

Learners are often aware of the problems raised by accent. Several students interviewed by Lynne Davies in Cardiff in 2006, for instance, felt they needed more help with listening work in class to aid their pronunciation and accent. On listening to a CD of the acclaimed language tutor Michel Thomas recently, I noticed how he stressed pronunciation in his simulated German lesson, asking the students to repeat specific words and phrases until he was satisfied with their utterances. I wondered if this emphasis on pronunciation and the attempt to virtually eliminate the learner's mother tongue accent when speaking a second language is the secret of Michel's success. Welsh learners are not always aware that their vowel sounds in particular 'o' and 'e' in Welsh can grate on Welsh-speakers. Gwilym Roberts, in his own inimitable way, gets learners to watch the shape of his mouth as he pronounces 'o'.

Sue Massey found that when she adopted a north Walian accent, Welsh-speakers did not tend to switch to English as much when she wished to practise Welsh. Judith Kaufmann, one of the four finalists in the Learner of the Year competition in 2002, said she had not experienced problems with using Welsh in Gwynedd:

Yn enwedig ar ôl y peth efo Dysgwr y Flwyddyn, roedd pawb yn siarad efo fi ar y stryd ac yn y bws: dach chi 'di gwneud mor dda. Roedden nhw hyd yn oed yn diolch i mi. Felly dw i ddim yn credu bod nhw ddim yn derbyn siaradwyr newydd yn eu plith o gwbl. Dw i wedi cael ymatebion cyfeillgar iawn.

(Especially after Learner of the Year, everyone was speaking to me on the street and on the bus. 'You've done so well.' They were even thanking me. So I do not think that they do not accept speakers amongst them. I have had very friendly responses.)

Her ready acceptance by local people may be due to the fact that they say she has an authentic accent and that her German accent is far less obvious when she speaks Welsh than when she speaks English.

It is rare for second-language speakers to lose their accents completely, but if they work on pronunciation and intonation from the beginning they should make themselves acceptable to Welsh-speakers. Jen Llywelyn offers wise advice:

WORK ON PRONUNCIATION FROM THE START! Everything depends on it! Be prepared to feel silly, but do it, get it right, and you will find everything is easier, and what's more, people will understand you!

Jen's tutor, Howard, stressed the importance of listening skills in helping to develop good pronunciation.

Pronunciation, intonation and accent are clearly an issue requiring attention on the part of learners, first-language speakers and tutors. If addressed adequately this could bring about a breakthrough in the number of learners who attain fluency

Welsh pronunciation is largely phonetic and any grammar or course book will explaine clearly how to pronounce Welsh. See for example *Teach Yourself Welsh Grammar*, by Christine Jones (Hodder

Headline, 2007) and *Teach Yourself Welsh Dictionary*, by Edwin Lewis (Hodder Headline, 2003). The main sounds that learners, particularly those from outside Wales, find difficult are listed below.

	PRONUNCIATION
dd as in *dydd* (day)	As the 'th' in the English word 'that'
ng as in *rhwng* (between)	As in the the English word 'gang'
ll as in *llaw* (hand)	Put the tip of the tongue just behind the top teeth and breathe out
th as in *gwaith* (work)	As the 'th' in the English word 'thanks'
r as in *car* (car)	It is very important to roll the 'r' in Welsh in order to sound natural. Learners tend to forget to do so, particularly at the end of words.
wy as in *pwy* (who)	Think of the English word 'gooey', remove the 'g' and say 'ooey' quickly
yw as in *byw* (to live)	Rhymes with 'eue' in the English word, 'queue'
o as in *glo* (coal)	It is difficult to find a similar sound in English but it is definitely not as in 'dough' but more like the 'oo' in the English word door.
e as in *ble* (where)	Another letter where it is difficult to find the equivalent sound in English. It is similar to the French word for tea – 'té'.
y as in '*dyn*' ('man') *y* as in '*llyn*' ('lake') *y* also as in *Cymru* (*Wales*)	As 'ee' in the English word 'deep' As 'i' in the English word 'tin' As 'u' in the English word 'up'

Ideally learners would benefit greatly from practising these sounds with first-language speakers, in particular the vowels 'o' and 'e' and rolling 'r'. If this is not possible, it is essential to listen carefully to CDs and the media.

Are they 'get by' learners?
The fact that many learners aim not to attain fluency but to 'get by' in the language further complicates the issue of Welsh-speakers' responses. Emyr Davies, WJEC's examination officer, believes that Welsh-speakers are more helpful if they realise someone is serious in their effort to learn, and this understanding is often linked with the knowledge that a student is preparing for an examination.

Of course, aims may change as learning progresses. Some students who initially only intended to gain a smattering of the language opt to become fluent and be fully integrated into a Welsh community. Many of them pass examinations. Others choose only to 'get by', whereas their initial aim was fluency. Such changes inevitably complicate first-language speakers' reactions to learners who are casual acquaintances as they are unsure of the learners' wishes and all but the most zealous are likely to use English rather than embarrass a diffident learner. On the basis of her research, Carol Trosset believes that:

> The real reason people do not speak Welsh to learners is that they have no real concept of a non-Welsh Welsh-speaker. They do not know what to do with learners, whether to treat them as Welsh or as English.

Expectations
Many first-language speakers then are totally flummoxed by learners. They don't know what to expect from them. Felicity Roberts, an experienced WfA tutor in Aberystwyth and one of the instigators of the *Cynllun Pontio* there, has noticed that first-language speakers have a clearer understanding of learners' potential after involvement with the scheme. Many first-language speakers have admitted to her that before participating in *Cynllun Pontio* they did not anticipate that they would be able to hold lengthy conversations with learners. First-language speakers clearly need time to adjust to the growing number of learners, as well as advice on how to support them in their attempt to use the language in the community. Meinir, from

Adrian Price hopes that first-language Welsh-speakers will respect the efforts people make to learn the language, and help them.

Aberystwyth told me that she has become more committed to helping learners since participating in the *Cynllun Pontio* scheme.

Adrian Price, Director of Teaching at the Welsh Language Teaching Centre for Adults at Cardiff University, believes learners are making a big effort to learn Welsh and hopes that Welsh-speakers will respect this and support them

---

Adrian's Top Tips to the *Cymry Cymraeg*

- Try to speak more slowly and clearly than usual
- Do not turn to English unless learners ask a question, because this can undermine learners' confidence.
- Don't worry. You are the mother-tongue speakers and the model to be imitated. You have the advantage every time.

'You can feel like you only have half a personality.' Why do learners switch?

Tiredness was a factor for some students who wrote journals, particularly for those with young children. The temptation was then very great to lapse into English. Stress may also decrease a learner's determination to keep speaking Welsh. When a close relative had been diagnosed with a serious illness, Alan reported feeling low and debilitated when trying to use Welsh, and sometimes wondered why he ever made the effort. Prior to this Alan had been particularly positive, learning quickly and practising regularly.

Some learners feel they cannot represent their true personality and intelligence when speaking in a language in which they are not fluent. Phyllis Kinney was acutely aware of this:

> Anything I had to say would be peppered with mistakes, and I am a lover of language. I love the process of choosing the precise word to bring out a subtle meaning, of turning a phrase in such a way as to shed a new light on a topic. And I knew that as far as the Welsh language was concerned I could not say what I *wanted* to say but what I was *able* to say.

Similarly Marilyn Lewis who learned Welsh in New Zealand in the 1980s, commented in her journal, 'My biggest lack is still not being able to sustain a normal conversation. Anything I can say is still determined by the words I know rather than by the ideas in my head.'

A learner interviewed as part of a research project by the WCC summed this up well: 'You become a child again, struggling to find the words in Welsh. If you transfer to English that power balance is even again, you aren't so vulnerable. Take away your ability to communicate effectively and you really are like a child.'

Expectancy and Insistence
First-language speakers' expectations clearly play an important role in inspiring learners to continue to use Welsh. Few first-language Welsh-speakers persisted in speaking Welsh to Mairi Higham, who admitted that, though eager to become fluent, she was reluctant to practise outside the classroom at first, and found it difficult to switch from English to Welsh, particularly with those she knew well. Both Mairi Higham and Pam Petro realise that this is not necessarily a problem that arises from reluctance on the Welsh-speaker's part, as the Welsh-speaker may sense that the learner has an ambivalent attitude to practice opportunities and may switch to English out of

kindness to alleviate the situation. Mairi tended to shy away from speaking to adults, finding it much easier to speak to young children, but found it extremely beneficial when she encountered Welsh-speakers who *expected* her to communicate in Welsh and *insisted* on speaking Welsh to her at all times. A breakthrough in fluency came when she moved from Cardiff to a traditional Welsh-speaking area in west Wales, and for five years was immersed in Welsh in the community and the workplace. She found it difficult during her first year in her new home to persist in speaking Welsh, but by the second year it became second nature. She returned to Cardiff a confident second-language speaker able to teach Welsh to adults and children; she also taught French through the medium of Welsh.

Students in many areas of Wales do not have such immersion opportunites. It is therefore of paramount importance that they are able to capitalise on every practice opportunity and are supported by Welsh-speakers who *expect* to hold a conversation with them.

The notion of expectancy was stressed by several students who wrote journals and mentioned by several others. Here's Alan again:

Nan from north Wales is a first-language Welsh-speaker. She *expects* me to speak Welsh, just as the staff at the nursery and school expect me to. At work I met up with Colin who used to be in my team. He is from Swansea and we always speak Welsh even though I struggle sometimes. It's this *expectation* bit again . . . I talked to the head teacher about Rick – now she never uses English. No, I can't remember a single occasion! Again, it is *her expectation* . . . I phoned Albert, who was a strong influence on my decision to learn Welsh. Again we have reached the point where *we expect* to speak Welsh together.

Athlete Tanni Grey-Thompson, a learner of Welsh.

Welsh-speakers' expectations then could be real motivators and encourage learners to persist when the inevitable ambivalence described by Mairi and Pam starts to surface. To quote Tanni again:

> If my parents had been different, if they had had low expectations for me, I could have grown up thinking very differently. But for me it was about having the chance to try, and seeing what I might achieve.

What can be done?

A picture emerges of many first-language speakers who find it difficult to help learners for a variety of reasons and consequently learners who become discouraged as they seek to practise and may even fear doing so. However, the role of first-language speakers is crucial and can be the catalyst that converts a learner into a second-language speaker. Noragh Jones makes the cardinal point, 'The first big breakthrough in learning the language comes, not when you achieve near perfection in a formal class but when the locals continue to speak Welsh in your presence.'

Peter McHarg, a learner from Inverness who now lives in Carmarthenshire, posted on the BBC website:

> . . . one of the most important (and nerve-racking) aspects of learning the language is practising. I am lucky to live in a largely Welsh first-language area and so have plenty of opportunity to practice. It is certainly a confidence boost when the locals feel comfortable enough to start a conversation with you in Welsh without feeling worried and embarrassed of you struggling to keep up.

It would seem that if first-language speakers know definitely that the learner wishes to practise, then practice may well take place successfully, but a problem will arise if the learner seems hesitant or if the first-language speaker is unsure how much the learner knows. When learners meet first-language speakers they do not know well, problems practising often occur for these reasons.

The world outside the classroom can be a frightening, confusing place for the learner and, even in homes where there are ready-made opportunities to practise, learners often stumble upon problems. Formal classes can provide help by preparing learners for what they should expect. But first-language speakers also need to be encouraged to adapt their speech when talking to learners, particularly in the early stages. Learners need help to appreciate many first-language speakers' concerns and the extra patience needed to converse with learners. One of the AWLP students, Rees, stressed at focus group, 'There is a cut-off point with Welsh-speakers when it becomes easier to speak English.'

He believes many Welsh-speakers fail to help learners as they have not had sufficient experience hearing learners use Welsh. This is changing as learners are making their presence felt more and more. Learners also need confidence to enable them to persist in times of difficulty. Tanni has valuable advice to offer:

Advice from Dame Tanni Grey-Thompson

You need self-belief. Although this may be challenged from time to time, really successful people are those who are able to deal with failure. Anyone can be successful once, but coming back from failure is a huge challenge, and one that not everyone wants to do, or can do. It means building on the hard days, when times are tough, and coming out the other side. You also of course have to learn to deal with success and not get carried away by it, believe that you are invincible.

Giving up is not an option

Some learners try to influence the behaviour of first-language speakers and others develop strategies to deal with hindrances that may occur when trying to use Welsh outside class. At the end of the day, however, the onus is on all learners to overcome any difficulties by sheer determination to succeed and by continuing to speak Welsh at every opportunity – even if the Welsh-speaker responds in English. Giving up should never be considered an option. Learners are not usually prepared for the gulf between learning in class and practising Welsh in the community, however. Perhaps more preparation by tutors before students practise outside class, as well as the advice in this book, could help more learners persevere, sustain their motivation to learn and develop powerful self-belief. As

Gwilym Roberts has stressed there needs to be determination on both sides if the situation is to improve. Learners must be determined to use Welsh at every opportunity and first-language speakers must rise to the challenge and provide the necessary support.

According to Elwyn Hughes, an experienced WfA tutor in south and north Wales, it takes guts!

The tutor Elwyn Hughes says learning
Welsh takes guts!

It takes guts!

Welsh learners are usually very keen to put their newly-learnt language skills into practice as soon as possible. They really psyche themselves up to pluck up the courage to say something like '*Ga' i frechdan ham, os gwelwch chi'n dda?*' (May I have a ham sandwich please?) in a café, only to feel totally demoralised when the waiter replies in English, 'White or brown bread?'

Well, it's not all bad news . . .

- You've been understood, so what you've learnt is making sense. A very big plus point.

- You know the waiter understands Welsh, so next time you'll be ready to carry on in Welsh even if he's responded to you in English. It takes guts to do that, but there's no escaping the fact that trying out your new language in any real life situation takes an awful lot of guts.
- If the waiter persists in speaking English, you'll know which café to boycott from now on. Finding the most learner-friendly café is infinitely more important than finding the tastiest ham sandwich.

Would you like to find out more?
Noragh Jones, *Living in Rural Wales* (Gomer, 1993)
Carol Trosset, *Welshness Performed* (Arizona Press, 1993)

Chapter 7
'Yes, cariad, be'chi mo'yn?'
Dialect, slang and elisions

Cymraeg Byw

In 1926 A. S. D. Smith, known as Caradar, an Englishman who taught languages in Blundell School, published a Welsh course, *Welsh Made Easy*, which presented the language in a clear and orderly manner. However, formal Welsh was used throughout, and it is doubtful whether anyone without a sound educational background and an understanding of the workings of grammar would be able to teach themselves everyday spoken Welsh using this textbook. Some of the learners who recorded their experiences in the interesting volume *Discovering Welshness* in 1992 paid tribute to Caradar's work, which had been largely responsible for their success. These were people of considerable educational background, able to teach themselves language from a conventional grammar book. Learning Welsh *formally* as an adult continued to be unusual in Wales in the early and mid-twentieth century, particularly for the non-intellectual, as the pioneering tutor Cennard Davies noted in 1999: *Ond hyd yn oed tua chanol y ganrif, roedd oedolion oedd wedi llwyddo i ddysgu'r Gymraeg yn dipyn o ryfeddod.* (But even around the middle of the twentieth century adults who had succeeded in learning the language were something of a wonder.)

The production of the first version of *Cymraeg Byw* in 1964 was the turning point in the unparalleled growth of learners over the ensuing decades. *Cymraeg Byw* is an attempt to define the main features of standard spoken Welsh, that is, the form of the language which lies somewhere between conservative literary Welsh on the one hand and the local regional dialects on the other. Bobi Jones published material to promote *Cymraeg Byw* among learners in the 1960s. He believes that mastery of the literary and dialectal forms can develop after communication skills are acquired. His book *Cymraeg i Oedolion* (1965) and the work of Dan L James, *Conversational Welsh* (1972) became increasingly popular. Eight thousand copies of *Conversational Welsh* were sold within three years of publication. The years following the adoption of *Cymraeg Byw* have been particularly fruitful in the field of Welsh learning.

Traditionally the variety of Welsh taught as a second language to both adults and children had been of a literary nature, bearing little similarity to the Welsh that learners heard outside the classroom. Little prominence was given to oral skills in examinations, and it was quite common for adults to have gained qualifications in Welsh and yet be unable to speak it. The problem of 'street cred' afflicted even the most capable. The scholar, poet and novelist, the late Rev Dr W T Pennar Davies is a classic example. Despite his outstanding ability in reading and writing Welsh he was very anxious about speaking Welsh when in school, and admitted that even after completing his degree in Cardiff University, 'I still could not speak Welsh and was too shy to venture.' Shortly afterwards he was coaxed into speaking Welsh by a friend at Oxford. After his marriage in 1943 to Rosemarie Wolff, a refugee from Nazi Germany, who learned Welsh very quickly, Welsh became the language of the home, and his children and grandchildren are Welsh-speaking.

Some eminent writers and scholars such as T Llew Jones and the late Ceinwen Thomas were dubious of the merits of *Cymraeg Byw*, viewing it as a synthetic language. However, as courses expanded in the 1960s and 1970s, providers and tutors realised the urgent need for the learners to be taught to *speak* the Welsh language, and *Cymraeg Byw* was increasingly used in classes. This change, together with the change in classroom methodology – the switch from the formal grammar translation method to using the communicative approach as the preferred method of teaching – helped learners to communicate more effectively outside class.

The 'bwlch' is great

While tutors attempt to expose learners to the Welsh they will meet in the community, there will inevitably be problems with dialect, low level registers, Welsh/English combinations, abbreviations, and levels of formality when learners first practise, for as Alan stressed at the focus group, 'The "bwlch" is great.' The use of dialect and slang may also be compounded by very rapid and poor articulation and elision, both live and on the media. This is the case with all second-language practice and use, the only exception being languages such as Cornish and Manx where everyone is a learner. Some years ago two teenagers from Germany stayed at my home and I was able to communicate well with them. However, when they were speaking just to each other it was very difficult for me to follow, presumably because they were using a combination of local dialect and the current teenage-speak. Similarly I found it impossible to understand much of what our Swiss neighbours were saying when they were chatting together in Swiss German, but I was able to communicate effectively with them in standard German. Learners often comment to tutors, 'They told me they don't say it as we say it in class.'

Children in Welsh-medium schools, whose parents are learning, often find it very difficult to accept that there could be another acceptable version of what teacher has said, so that any slight deviation, be it dialect or standard speech, from what they have learned at school may well mean that they will refuse to use Welsh with their parents.

Lynne Evans attended an intensive course at Aberystwyth shortly after her attempts at private study failed to really help her. However, when she first began to use Welsh *yn y byd mawr* (in the real world), memorising patterns from course dialogues that would equip her for this task, she was dismayed that a shopkeeper, unfamiliar with the learners' classroom uttered, '*Yes, cariad, be'chi mo'yn?*' (Yes, dear, what do you want?) instead of *Gaf i eich helpu chi*? (May I help you?), the standard form learned in class. This was the first of many such experiences, but Lynne was determined and gradually adapted her classroom Welsh to that generally used in her locality. Strong motivation conquers all obstacles, and she persevered until she became a fluent speaker.

Dialect issues can be particularly troublesome for learners who try to practise when away from their home area. In the 1990s Steve Morris recorded examples of learners' attempts to converse with Cymry Cymraeg being totally thwarted, because they used sentence patterns which were not identical to the local dialect. This situation places tutors and course organisers in a dilemma as to how much dialect to include in courses. There are a number of dialects in Welsh but the chief dividing line is between the north and south. However, it would be too simplistic to give the impression that Wales has only two dialects: many differences exist in other regions.

While course books are produced in north- and south-Walian versions, it is not possible to include all dialectal variations or slang, nor indeed would it be beneficial to learners. WLPAN intensive courses vary considerably in the north, south and west of Wales, but again do not cover all the dialect versions of the patterns learnt. There are dialect variations in vocabulary, sounds and sentence structure, and it would be discouraging in the extreme for learners to be taught so many different versions when learning basic language patterns. When a degree of fluency has been reached it is time to become au fait with the dialects and cross the bridge to become a fully-fledged second-language speaker. Most first-language speakers are aware of the differences and with a little effort could accommodate learners. They know that when a learner says, for example, *'chwarae teg'* (fair play) it is the standard form of *ware teg,* which they use in dialect, or when the learner says *gwybod* or *adnabod* (words for 'know' in Welsh) these are the standard forms of *gwpod* or *napod* used in some areas of south Wales. North Walians are aware of the different vocabulary and constructions used in the south. Constructions such as *Mae gen i blentyn* (I have a child) in the north correspond to *Mae plentyn gyda fi* in the south, but both forms are clear to the vast majority of *Cymry Cymraeg.*

The first-language speaker's accent may also be a stumbling block to a learner, particularly if dialect is also used and the learner is practising away from home. This hindrance is particularly difficult to overcome, as while first-language speakers can accommodate other registers of Welsh, it would not be so easy to adapt their accents. Speaking slowly could help, however.

In the light of on-going controversy about the standard of Welsh used by the media, it was interesting that learners wrote in journals that they did not like slang or Welsh-English combinations. Rees commented, *'Hanner awr yn gwrando ar "Pam fi Duw", anodd i ddilyn y jôcs er gwaetha'r "Wenglish".* Mae gormod o "Wenglish".' (Half an hour of listening to 'Why me, God', difficult to follow the jokes despite the 'Wenglish'. There is too much 'Wenglish'.)

And Laura, who moved to Gwynedd to work when she was recording her experiences in the journal wrote:

When I try to speak Welsh people don't seem to understand me at first and I have to try again – it could just be that they are expecting me to speak English! Some people have said to me that it is daft to use 'proper Welsh' and told me I should use English words instead of the Welsh. Personally I think that, as a learner, I should try not to mix the two languages and that Welsh should be kept as pure as possible (if you know what I mean?!?) I actually find it more difficult when people use Wenglish as I get more lazy when I'm listening because you can get the gist of the conversation from all the English words! I find it easier to understand up here than when I lived in Cardiff and I'm very glad that I have had lessons in both the south and north versions of Welsh as it has helped me understand a wider variety of people.

Laura commented to me that people she already knows are very helpful but casual acquaintances use 'regional slang', which she finds very difficult.

Philip felt passionately that 'Wenglish' should be avoided. At a focus group he expressed disappointment that Welsh-speakers frequently use concocted words such as *'mantelpils'* for mantelpiece when they could be using the Welsh *'silff ben tân'*. Such habits frustrate learners, who are trying to acquire as much vocabulary as possible, he believes and thinks Welsh-speakers should always use the correct words and use a dictionary if there is any uncertainty.

Interestingly, Hilda Hunter and Caroline Williams considered that too much slang is used on WfA courses. They believe this will eventually result in a general deterioration in the standard of the language spoken in Wales and call for correct Welsh to be used in all classes. However, shortly after their book was published Helen Prosser appeared on *S4C* news. She explained that research has shown that Welsh-speakers are more willing to communicate with learners who use colloquial Welsh and have a good accent than with those who speak very correctly but have poor pronunciation. Once the basics have been mastered then it is a good idea for learners to try to adapt to their area.

Steve Morris stresses that learners should not think that spoken Welsh that is different to what was learned in class is 'incorrect' or 'substandard' in any way. It is just different, and taking an active interest in it will be appreciated by local Welsh-speakers. In order to do this, Steve advises making a note of words and grammatical patterns used in the learner's area that are different from words learned in class, and to pay particular attention to pronunciation and incorporate it into the learner's speech. Sometimes you hear the 'au', used for the plural form of many nouns, as an 'a' or an 'e' sound.

Steve advises:

Peidiwch â phoeni. Rhowch gynnig arni.
(Don't worry. Give it a go)

Mixed messages

Sometimes learners get contradictory messages from Welsh-speakers. Pat Metcalfe, a confident learner in west Wales, has found this quite harassing:

Pan ffrind a fi wedi mynd i Gwrs Gloywi Cymraeg yn Llanbed roedden ni'n arfer mynd i gaffi am baned. Yn sgwrsio gyda pobl eraill, 'Rydyn ni wedi ymddeol,' dwedes i. 'O, na, na, na!' daeth yr ateb – 'Wedi RITIRO.' Y tro nesaf, 'wedi ritiro' dwedes i. 'O, na, na, na! – wedi YMDDEOL,' dwedodd y ddynes. Ych a fi!
(When a friend and I went on a *Cwrs Gloywi Cymraeg* in Lampeter we used to go to a café for a cuppa. On chatting with other people, 'We have retired' I said (using the word 'ymddeol'). 'O, no, no, no' came the response: 'Retired!' using 'RITIRO.' The next time I said 'wedi ritiro'. 'O, no, no, no! – wedi YMDDEOL,' said the lady.' Ugh!)

Probably the first-language speaker was not aware that she had caused any confusion but as learners' confidence can easily plummet, thoughtless comments may cause discouragement.

Gogs and Hwntws

Some AWLP students really struggled with dialect. Here's Rees again:

> *Ron i'n siarad wrth ymwelwr i'r swyddfa ond newidiodd i Saesneg achos 'mod i'n ffeindio ei dafodiaith yn anodd. Dyn o Sir Gâr, mae'n bosib.*
>
> (I was speaking to a visitor in the office and he changed to English because I found his dialect difficult. A man from Carmarthenshire possibly.)

Others wanted to learn more dialect in order to communicate with Welsh-speakers, but only dialects that were likely to come across regularly.

> *Dw i'n teimlo'n iawn yn siarad Cymraeg gyda'r pobl o'r de neu gorllewin achos bod teulu fy ngŵr yn dod o Tŷ Ddewi ... Ond dw i'n anhapus iawn yn siarad gyda 'Gogs'. Dwi i'n credu bod e'n iaith wahanol iawn iawn!! Weithiau, dw i'n meddwl fy mod i'n gwella ac bydda i'n rhugl a wedyn dw i'n glywed pobl gogledd yn y stryd a dw i'n meddwl 'Wel, wnes i ddim deall un gair.'*
>
> (I feel fine speaking Welsh with people from the south and the west because my husband's family come from St. David's ... But I am unhappy speaking with north Walians. I think that it is a very very different language!! Sometimes, I think that I am improving and I will be fluent and then I hear north Walians in the street and think 'Well, I didn't understand one word.')

Kim volunteered at focus group that it is sometimes difficult to follow dialect in one's first language, which means learners face an almost impossible task when they first try using Welsh outside class if first-language speakers respond with dialect and slang. She had picked up some west Walian dialect from her in-laws and was disappointed when a tutor rebuked her for using it in class. Her regular tutor encourages the students to extend their knowledge in discussions including dialect as well as standard forms.

It works both ways, of course, as Mark from Bangor noted in a blog in June, 2006:

south-Walian is very confusing; once someone from Cardiff spoke to me in [his] Welsh and I could hardly understand a word! Although, I have received a lot of praise and respect for learning Welsh – especially because I am a *Sais*! (Englishman).

For one AWLP student, Lydia, however, the use of dialect and Welsh/English combinations was encouraging in a somewhat convoluted way. When interviewed she said that she has great difficulty in understanding Welsh-speakers and thinks this is probably because they use dialect. She said she felt encouraged when trying to follow television programmes such as *Pobl y Cwm*, as she has noticed on occasions that when an English or Welsh/English combination word is used she often knows the correct Welsh word.

Immersion – the best option
Some learners are able to immerse themselves in the language of the community and workplace and adapt quickly to using dialect and Welsh/English combinations. Mairi Higham, for example, said *Cymrâg*, not *Cymraeg*, for Welsh, and often used words and expressions used locally such as *bennu* instead of *gorffen* (finish) or *joio* instead of *mwynhau* (enjoy) when she lived in west Wales. She realised however that the grounding she had received in classes gave her the foundation on which to build her independent learning. Although she was willing to adapt her Welsh in this way and understood that some local people, particularly the elderly, did not feel comfortable using words such as *trydan* (electricity) or *cyfrifiadur* (computer) she did not use grammatically incorrect Welsh that was prevalent in the area, such as *Mae e ddim* for *Dydy e ddim* (he isn't) or tolerate children who used patterns such as, '*On i'n really geto along gyda teacher cello fi*', which hardly needs translating. Adapting to local usage, as Mairi did, means that a fluent learner blends in with the crowd and may become indistinguishable from a first-language speaker if they have good pronunciation, intonation and accent.

Spot the Difference
Huw Lewis, who researched the motives and attitudes of learners on an intensive WLPAN in Lampeter in 2001, believes that in his own

experience, and that of first-language speakers known to him, it is almost invariably possible to differentiate between a learner and a first-language speaker. Paedar Morgan, a tutor from Inverness, has made the same point about Gaelic learners and first-language speakers in Scotland. Most of the Welsh learners Huw interviewed at the intensive course were aware of this, and he could only point to one learner as an exception, a shopkeeper, who though an in-migrant was indistinguishable from locals. When asked how he had managed it, the shopkeeper said it was the result of living in the community for seventeen years and for twelve of those trying to forget everything he had been taught in Welsh class.

While immersion in the language of the local community is vital, a foundation in the language acquired in class is a good springboard for a learner. Possibly the shopkeeper reached his conclusions, which I suspect are presented almost 'tongue in cheek', as a result of hearing learners persist in using expressions from class in the community and not extending their vocabulary or adapting to the local dialect so that they are labelled by locals as using 'learners' Welsh' or 'WLPAN Welsh'.

A similar situation takes place in Israel where in-migrant Hebrew learners are often able to survive by finding a job using their first-language or English. They may continue to move almost exclusively within their own ethnic group; even after completion of an ULPAN, they often have a limited 'ULPAN vocabulary', which means they cannot hold a conversation of any depth or understand the media and never fully integrate with Hebrew-speakers.

I wonder how many fully-integrated Welsh-language learners there are – perhaps more than we realise. After all if they are indistinguishable from first-language speakers, only those who there are familiar with their background know that they have learned Welsh. Marika Fusser from Germany, who lives and works in Gwynedd says that when she rings someone and speaks in English she is asked often, *'Cymraeg ydych chi?'* Barbara Owsianka from Poland, who featured on *O Flaen dy Lygaid* in June 2007, also sounds as if she belongs in Gwynedd. The experience of a fluent learner in Aberystwyth originally from England also makes me wonder whether there are some learners who are taken for first-language speakers by everyone except those who know them well: someone complained to her about the English coming to heartland areas taking the jobs that belonged to Welsh people. It was assumed that she was a first-language Welsh-speaker and would be bemoaning the same issue! Learners need the class just as a child needs parents, but just as the child gradually becomes independent, so does the learner who seeks fluency and integration.

Speaking 'in a code'

Elisions, the omission of a final or initial sound in pronunciation, may also harass learners. Agnes complained, 'Modern Welsh is too abbreviated.' Elisions frustrate Agnes as she has a good grasp of the traditional grammatical formations. Similarly Rees stressed at interview that one of his main problems was recognising what Welsh-speakers say. He, like Agnes has an excellent grasp of Welsh grammar and a very wide vocabulary. 'Welsh-speakers often leave words out – key words – and seem to speak in a code.'

Rees contrasts how easy it is for him to read and write Welsh compared to the struggle he experiences when he tries to converse. Some Welsh-speakers have told him he speaks well, but he expects more of himself. Listening and understanding are even a problem for him in class, but more so in 'the real world'. Interestingly Agnes and Rees, the students who most stressed the problem with elisions, were the two who reported very little Welsh-speaking practice in their journals. They are readers who do not really aspire to become fluent speakers despite their knowledge. In fact Rees had been pressurised by his employer to attend a class that majored on speaking skills, and Agnes said she considered it an impossibility to become a fluent speaker, but enjoyed reading Welsh and wanted to build on her reading skills.

Issues of dialect, slang and elisions are not easy ones to resolve and are challenging for some learners. It is not surprising that Noragh Jones commented, 'No wonder they say the learner's biggest problem is understanding what people say back.' However, with persistence, learners will become au fait with the local dialect and gradually sound more like a first-language speaker.

A tip from a world expert
With patience on the part of the learner and the first-language speaker, over time communication should become easier. Earl Stevick, author of over forty books on language learning, believes that repeatedly listening to and producing the same material with a first-language speaker is particularly useful. He finds it beneficial to tell something to a speaker of the language and have that person tell the same thing back to him in correct, natural form. He then repeats the same material again, bearing in mind the way he has just heard it. This could be repeated several times. Obviously, availability of first-language speakers and their willingness to help is essential for this routine. It could be particularly useful for learners with ready-made practice partners at home who could give five or ten minutes a day to such an activity. However, anyone can familiarise themselves with the local dialect by a combination of listening carefully to those around them, and by studying the books on dialect recommended below.

Would you like to find out more?
There are two useful books for learners who would like to know more about Welsh dialects, but many learners will be able to imbibe the local variations by imitation:

Beth Thomas and Peter Wynn Thomas, *Cymraeg, Cymrâg, Cymrêg . . . Cyflwyno'r Tafodieithoedd* (Gwasg Taf, 1989: out of print but available in libraries)
Alan R. Thomas, *Welsh Dialect Survey*, (University of Wales Press, 2000)

you CAN speak Welsh

Chapter 8
'No "gissernuvvering" and no "turbo Welsh" please!' – Speed

The speed of first-language speakers' speech, an issue very closely related to the use of dialect, slang and elisions, is often problematic for second-language learners. Edward Enfield, in his engaging book *Greece on My Wheels*, makes some astute comments on this matter:

> Now it is my belief that the Linguaphone course never teaches the language it purports to teach, it teaches something else, which should be called a Lingua-language. Lingua-French and Lingua-German are, I am quite sure, different from the languages that they speak in France and Germany. They are a great deal nicer for a start. If you learn Lingua-English you would say, in carefully modulated tones, such things as 'Please may I have another one,' whereas the first-language population say 'C'd ivor nuther' or possibly 'Gisser nuvver.' I therefore go about Greece asking carefully for another one, at which all the Greeks are greatly surprised, as they are gissernuvvering.

Meinir, a first-language speaker volunteered, '*Mae siaradwyr Cymraeg yn siarad yn rhy gyflym. Fel athrawes plant bach rwy'n siarad yn bwyllog.*' (Welsh-speakers speak too quickly. As a teacher of young children I speak clearly and steadily.) The AWLP students came across 'gissernuvvering' Welsh-speakers. Laura complained that, while Welsh-speakers known to her spoke at an acceptable speed, she often found the pace of unfamiliar Welsh-speakers demoralizing. Similarly, Rees said that some Welsh-speakers seemed oblivious to his limitations and spoke so rapidly he became lost. Sharon was disappointed that the rapid speech of first-language speakers sometimes resulted in unnecessary language switching. Welsh-speakers, in her opinion, needed to allow more time for the learner to work out what has been said and to devise an answer. Similarly, Philip found that, even though Welsh-speakers are supportive, they tend to speak speedily and at great length. As a result, he often loses the thread, another reason for both parties to switch to English. Agnes found the issue of 'speed' particularly harassing and linked it with the issue of elisions. Sioned wrote at length on the pace of Welsh-speakers' speech:

> My friend came to visit from the north of England and we went to meet one of his friends. She automatically started to speak to me in Welsh, so I said in Welsh that I was learning but I couldn't speak Welsh. She looked very surprised. I think when people hear my name they expect me to speak Welsh. In the evening she was speaking Welsh in front of us with her friends. . . . They were speaking quite quickly or it seemed they were speaking quickly. This is not the type of conversation where you can join in . . . It's much easier talking to a Welsh learner especially someone who is roughly on the same level as you because they don't expect too much of you and know how you feel when you are trying to speak Welsh, i.e. having to put in lots of bits of English and expecting to mess things up quite often. You're very willing to help one another out. Sometimes when you're speaking to a fluent Welsh-speaker you feel that they are getting impatient even when they are probably not and I quite often feel that they are expecting me to be better than I am. This is why sometimes if someone asks me something in Welsh I will answer in English because I don't want to let the other person down.

Sioned realises that first-language speakers are not necessarily speaking particularly quickly or becoming impatient, and that much of the problem can be attributed to the fact that learners are straining to understand each word. This is a state of affairs in which it is easy to assign blame, but where insight is required by both parties. While it is easier on one level to practise with other learners in the long term this will not help you 'cross the bridge' to become a second-language speaker.

Interestingly, a learner from overseas, Anna, whom I interviewed at the Eisteddfod, praised Welsh-speakers for their help and said they spoke especially slowly for her.

The speed of first-language speakers' speech can be a particular problem for advanced learners, as Alan says: 'They start slowly, but forget you're a learner and speed up.'

Kim was worried as her young son spoke so quickly to her husband – a first-language speaker – she often needed to ask him to translate for her. Welsh-speakers may treat advanced learners as first-language speakers as they forget, or fail to realise, their limitations. Advanced learners may feel more diffident to ask Welsh-speakers to reduce their speed of speech as they feel more is expected of them than of students at beginner or intermediate level.

Annabel recorded a conversation she had with a Welsh-speaking mother at her children's school, 'She spoke slowly at first. She repeated the sentence if I asked her to or a word if I did not understand the meaning. The more she talked the faster she talked. There were some words or phrases I did not understand, e.g. Welsh for 'probably'. I find it difficult to picture the word if I haven't already learnt it.'

There are reports from many other sources too, for instance the WCC study in 2005 when several students reported they found it difficult to keep up with first-language speakers. One student said, 'They speak 'turbo' Welsh, it's hard to keep up.'

Some students blamed themselves if they could not cope with the speed of speech of first-language speakers. For example, a student interviewed for a research project by Haydn Hughes commented: '*Mae bai arna i. Does dim digon o hyder gyda fi achos maen nhw'n siarad yn gyflym.*' (It's my fault. I don't have enough confidence because they speak quickly.)

As with the issue of dialect, speed is not an easy one to solve and it could be that the differences in word order between sentences in English and Welsh make life more difficult for learners. If learners ask Welsh-speakers to repeat and speak slowly rather than turn to English, progress will be made over time. Unless learners speak up about matters that hinder their progress in using Welsh outside class, first-language speakers will not be made aware of their needs. Following the media regularly may also help and of course concentrating on listening to first-language speakers at every opportunity possible – even if they think you are eavesdropping!

Chapter 9
'When you can use Welsh in the bank you know you've made it.' Welsh in the workplace

It's easier just socialising with colleagues

Many learners are happy socialising in Welsh but hesitant about using Welsh at work. This is a situation that has been changing gradually over the last fifteen years. Since the passing of the 1993 Welsh Language Act, which requires that all public bodies give equal status to Welsh and English, numbers of 'Welsh in the Workplace' courses have increased quite rapidly. This is an important step in the revitalisation of the language, as scholars argue that there is a link between the struggle to establish Welsh as the language of work and the increase in its prestige value. However, these pioneering schemes in the workplace have sometimes generated problems and been subject to a higher drop-out rate than other classes.

Staff from the Department of Engineering, Cardiff University, on their workplace Welsh course.

One of the main problems is lack of confidence in using Welsh in a workplace setting, even among those who speak fairly fluently. All the AWLP students, even those attending workplace courses, said at interviews that they preferred using the language socially at or outside work to working through the medium of Welsh. Surprisingly this even applied to Clare: though the initial trigger had been a request from an employer to learn Welsh, she found that she was enjoying using the language with friends and with her children.

Another problem on workplace courses is the irregular attendance of some students because of conflicting work demands. Learners may then become discouraged about their progress and cease learning. Courses are rarely very intensive and usually take place before or after work, or during the lunch hour. Other problems are linked with the status of learners in the workplace. A student in a managerial role, for instance, may feel threatened if he or she has limited time to devote to learning and practising and notices a junior colleague making faster progress. This is particularly so when speaking in class, and may also result in students giving up.

Can you really talk about technical issues in Welsh?
Using Welsh in the workplace was viewed as virtually unattainable by all at focus groups, even Alan, who has passed *Defnyddio'r Gymraeg Uwch* (the equivalent of an 'A' level). Students agreed that they are anxious about making mistakes at work and saw Welsh only as a language to use socially with colleagues. Indeed Sioned volunteered that in her workplace Welsh-speakers and learners did not want their superiors to know about their Welsh skills, as their employer sometimes asked Welsh-speakers to appear on the media as spokespeople, and the staff were already under pressure without such additional demands. Sioned and Alice stressed that they would be too anxious about causing misunderstandings if working through the medium of Welsh. Kim also stressed how difficult it would be to transfer her Welsh skills to her workplace as the work was of a technical nature. Interestingly, however, she appeared on the television programme *Welsh in a Week* two years after the focus groups took place, and was discussing her work in Welsh. Rees struggles when using Welsh orally at work but has no problem with written work. Agnes, now retired, said she would not have had

sufficient confidence to use Welsh at work as she, too, is far more confident reading than speaking. Her work was of a technical nature and she would fear making mistakes and causing problems as a result.

Gareth, a first-language speaker had experienced this first hand, '*O dro i dro, rwy'n siarad gyda trydanwr sy'n gweithio yn y brifysgol. Y broblem ydy fod angen trafod stwff gweddol gymhleth – a mae yn duedd i droi i'r Saesneg.*' (From time to time I speak to an electrician in the University. The problem is that sometimes it is necessary to discuss quite complicated stuff – and there is a tendency to turn to English.)

Philip, Sharon and Andrea thought it feasible to use Welsh in a school or nursery setting and Andrea and Sharon are already doing so with young children as volunteers at *Ysgol Feithrin*. As Welsh has penetrated education for many decades now it probably does not seem so frightening for learners, whereas other workplace settings such as business, medical or legal were viewed by learners as a particularly high accomplishment and practically unachievable even for first-language speakers. However, this could well be fear of the unknown, for as yet Welsh has not penetrated these domains substantially.

You can say anything in Welsh
Learners and first-language speakers alike often fail to recognize Welsh as a language to be used in the business domain or for technical work, a problem deeply rooted in history. Since the sixteenth century when English became the official language of administration as a result of the Act of Union with England in 1536, the Welsh language has been limited to predominantly cultural and social spheres and used minimally in commercial fields. English gradually came to be seen as the language of authority, whereas Welsh was the language of domesticity. Such innate attitudes cannot change overnight, particularly as they embody deep rooted feelings of inferiority, which may well have had a negative effect on the self-esteem of Welsh people. It was not always so. For two centuries after the Norman conquest, Welsh remained the language of law, government and culture in Wales, whereas French had become the language in those domains in England. Welsh was the official language in the Medieval period and had status throughout society, being used in all domains and competing with Latin as the language

of religion. In the tenth century the laws of Wales were codified in Welsh as well as Latin. However, it is widely held that because modern Welsh has not fulfilled a wide range of functions for several centuries, it is thus incapable of doing so.

Wales in the lead

Welsh terms in the business world and in specialist fields such as law, science and dentistry have been coined in recent years. Subjects such as education, administration, human resources, legislation, retail terminology, shop signs, food menus, finance and highways are included in the Welsh National Database of Terms, downloadable from the WLB's website. As time goes by, more and more specialized terms will be provided with Welsh equivalents by language experts. Interestingly, unlike other European languages that generally use American English for media and computer terminology, Welsh has coined its own words for television (*teledu*), computer (*cyfrifiadur*), internet (*rhyngrwyd*), website (*wefan*) and mobile phone (*ffôn symudol*). In 2006 the WLB launched a glossary for the information technology (IT) generation, which includes words for all essential IT usage such as cookies (*cwcis*) and lap top (*gliniadur*). Predictive texting in Welsh was launched in 2006. In May 2008 OfCom's regional communications market report indicated that there are now over 14,000 Wikipedia articles in Welsh, more than twice as many as the number in Gaelic – significant considering that Wales has a lower rate of broadband take-up than the rest of the UK.

Hopefully, innovations such as these will help to bring about more positive attitudes to the use of Welsh in the workplace and aid first-language speakers and learners alike, so that attitudes of surprise and fear associated with using Welsh will gradually disappear.

Workplace Successes

Pamela Petro was forced into writing a cheque in Welsh in the bank in Patagonia as there was no other way of communicating. She regarded her success as a particular achievement. 'When you can use Welsh at the bank you know you've made it.' It may take a generation or two but such attitudes are likely to change over time as Welsh is increasingly used.

Despite prejudices and fears about the use of Welsh in the

workplace, and a myriad of practical problems that may hinder students attending regularly, there have been many successful workplace ventures. There are testimonies from learners who have been immersed in a Welsh-speaking workplace setting and have benefited from the experience. Eirwen Gardner learned Welsh as an adult, but confidence to use the language naturally only developed when she obtained a post with a drama company and was required to work through the medium of Welsh. *'Mae'r profiad o weithio yn Gymraeg wedi bod yn werthfawr iawn i mi. Mae angen mwy o swyddi i ddysgwyr.'* (The experience of working in Welsh has been valuable for me. More jobs for learners are needed.)

Lila Haines reported similar experiences, and believes it is important to be able to communicate with people in the language of their choice when they contact an organisation. This is particularly important when people's emotions are affected, for example in a hospital or social work setting. The late June Barnes, a social worker, who learned Welsh as an adult, found that her knowledge of Welsh, though limited, was a great comfort to a Welsh-speaking family, who found difficulty expressing themselves in English. Over years June developed her language skills to such a level that she could use Welsh confidently in the workplace but admitted that it had taken an immense effort be able to work through her second language.

Nid ar chwarae bach y dysgwch chi iaith newydd, yn arbennig os ydy'r iaith yn iaith leafrifol fel y Gymraeg. June Barnes
(It is no light thing to learn a new language, especially a lesser-used one such as Welsh.)

There have also been reports of first-language speakers, for example when in hospital, valuing staff who are learners using some Welsh, even if their knowledge is not advanced enough to discuss medical issues. However, the present situation is a far cry from there being Welsh available for all Welsh-speakers to speak to medical/caring personnel in all areas of Wales.

Some organisations are particularly proactive in promoting Welsh in the workplace. A south Wales bank, for example, is committed to producing bilingual employees. *Canolfan Byd Gwaith* (Job Centre Plus) presents awards each year at the National

Eisteddfod to learners who have made outstanding progress in using Welsh in the workplace. Gwynedd County Council have also recognized the hard work of staff who learn Welsh by awarding two prizes annually since 1999, one for those who have made the most progress over a twelve month period, and one for those who have 'crossed the bridge' from being a second-language learner to a second-language speaker in a twelve month period.

There are rôle models in a variety of workplace spheres: for instance several Assembly Members who have learned Welsh use it in the chamber. A particularly inspiring rôle model in north Wales is the out-going chief constable of Gwynedd, Richard Brunstrom, now a fluent second-language speaker, who believes in leading by example. He became a high-ranking member of the *Gorsedd* at the National Eisteddfod in 2006 in recognition of his services to the language.

Workplace Welsh, then, is an area of great potential, and one where many hindrances and prejudices need to be overcome. It is not surprising that many learners who use Welsh socially are diffident about Welsh in the workplace, as many fluent first-language speakers are also hesitant about using professionally. Gwen Awbery, formerly co-ordinating lecturer for Welsh at the Department of Lifelong Learning, Cardiff University, has noticed that more Welsh-speakers are attending courses to improve their language skills since the 1993 Act and the formation of the National Assembly for Wales. She recommends that learners be content with half-way houses at first, using Welsh socially, and some of the time in the workplace, and then gradually building up to use Welsh in all settings as ability and confidence develop.

Steve Morris advises wearing a badge displaying the *Iaith Gwaith* logo in the workplace to show a willingness to use Welsh. The use of the *Iaith Gwaith* logo on badges, counters, in shop windows and in the workplace generally shows customers, clients, employers and employees that Welsh services are available. It would be good if Welsh-speakers and learners wore such badges outside the workplace too as this would encourage more conversations. A Welsh-speaker or learner could be sitting next to someone on a bus or in a waiting room and would only realise they could converse in Welsh if they saw a badge.

Steve Morris advises all learners to take a more active role in using Welsh in the business world. Learners in the past have made a difference in the workplace, and there is a potential for future learners to build on these successes. This will only happen when prejudices are broken down and where employers are proactive and supportive.

Another tip from Steve Morris
Many businesses offer dedicated Welsh language customer services.

- Make a pledge to yourself that from now on, you will always use the Welsh language service.
- Don't forget, you are the customer and you are making the choice of which language to use.
- As with everything else, don't worry if you don't know the standard Welsh word for something: do what everybody else does and use the English word!

Chapter 10
Crossing the 'other' bridge – culture and identity

'To know another language is to have a second soul.'
Charlemagne, King of the Franks (742-814)

A new dimension

As their knowledge of Welsh grows many learners become increasingly aware of other dimensions in the language learning process. They successfully cross the bridge to fluency only to find another bridge on the horizon:

Dim ond man cychwyn yw'r iaith a bod cymaint yn rhagor i'w ddysgu cyn dechrau deall y bobl.
(The language is only a starting point and there is as much and more to learn before starting to understand the people.)
Lynne Evans, 1989

The linguist Robert Gardner believes that learning a language is different from learning most other subjects, as it involves making something foreign a part of one's self. Any learner who wants more than a smattering of the language and whose ultimate aim is fluency will inevitably stumble upon issues of culture and identity, for these are matters that are not easily disentangled from language. Indeed languages are channels of culture, and open doors to invisible worlds where multiple treasures lie in wait to captivate and motivate learners – but sometimes unsettle them and generate disquiet.

Identity, an issue closely related to culture and with the need to belong, comes to the fore as learners progress. But what is 'a Welsh identity'? What is 'Welshness' and can a fluent learner really belong and become Welsh? Do all learners want such involvement? Do Welsh-speakers want learners to belong?

113

A new world

There are countless examples in the (auto)biographical literature of Welsh learners in which they realise they must tackle dimensions other than the linguistic as they venture into the community, and there is an almost universal awareness that by doing so they would be enriched. For Lois Martin-Short, using Welsh outside class opened up a new understanding of the area where she lived and its people, '*Mae dysgu Cymraeg wedi bod yn debyg i agor drws. Yn sydyn gallwn i weld pethau a phobl oedd yn anweledig o'r blaen a hefyd gallen nhw fy ngweld i.*' (Learning Welsh has been like opening a door. Suddenly I can see things and people that were invisible previously and they can see me.)

And for Alice Traille James who has settled in Crymych:

> Your whole world is enriched when you speak another language and it is important for people moving into Welsh-speaking areas to learn Welsh so that they understand the place they have come to live and the people who live there. It is not just a language that you learn and understand but an ancient culture that is full of things like the *eisteddfodau* and *cynghanedd*. It is so much more than just a language and it has helped me to set down new roots here.

Like the German-born Egyptologist and writer, Kate Bosse Griffiths, who learned Welsh in the 1930s in order to read and write Welsh literature, Lois, Alice and many others realized that knowing the language brought them nearer to the soul of the Welsh people.

A new identity

At the beginning of the book we viewed the revival of interest in Welsh language and culture as part of a global picture, a desire for integration within a community, a small unit that generates a sense of belonging and comradeship. A report by Her Majesty's Inspectors in 1984 noted that prominent in almost every class of adults learning Welsh were those seeking to regain a language not transmitted to them by a previous generation. Amid the anonymity of modern life, the Welsh-speaking world can provide a security, that sense of belonging that the UK has lost as community spirit dwindles.

When Alan attended an English literature course in the early 1990s he heard the tutor speak Welsh during the break and experienced a strange feeling of being *'outside'*. It was then he became determined to learn Welsh and also to send his young son to Welsh school. Sylvia Prys Jones, a fluent Welsh learner, spoke of the significance for her of belonging to a Welsh community. A lover of languages, who found all she studied easy, she was particularly captivated by Welsh as it was 'not just a language but an identity'. Sylvia speaks for many adult learners when describing Welsh language and culture as, 'a bulwark against the flood of the monolithic, vapid Anglo-American culture that has swept through our country in recent decades.' She comments on articles that appeared in the press when she was learning, which claimed that the majority of learners were people for whom Welsh was a crutch as it gave them the security of belonging. She cannot understand why that is often seen as something to be despised and fails to see the problem critics of learners have, as it is surely no crime to want to belong and have roots. She believes, however, that though she will never quite be 'really Welsh', her children will be, for they have been brought up in Welsh-medium education in a Welsh heartland area.

John Barnie, another fluent learner, believes that as culture and language are inseparable and both bound up in the expression of individuality, with his background, even as a Welsh learner living in a Welsh heartland area for many years, he will never 'become' Welsh: 'Thirteen years in Denmark taught me that, for most, the language you are brought up in is the water in which you must swim.' Oliver Davies, on the other hand, believed he became 'really Welsh' when he mastered the language.

What is 'Welshness'?
There are many strands of 'Welshness'. The actor, Ali Yassine, a fluent second-language speaker and WfA tutor is surely right in saying that being Welsh is something indefinable that exists in the heart of individual. Here's Ali's comment:

Dysgais i siarad Cymraeg oherwydd fy mod i eisiau fy hunaniaeth fy hun. Cefais fy magu yn hanner Eifftwr, hanner Somali, ond byth heb fod yn sicr os mai'r naill neu'r llall oeddwn i oherwydd nad oeddwn yn gallu siarad y naill iaith neu'r llall. Tybais trwy ddysgu Cymraeg y byddwn yn cadarnhau fy hunaniaeth, ond yna sut mae diffinio beth yw bod yn Gymro? Nid wyf i'n credu mai daeryddiaeth, na iaith, na lliw sy'n diffinio hunaniaeth rhywun. Yn hytrach rhywbeth yng nghalonnau pob un ohonyum ydyw.

(I learnt to speak Welsh because I wanted an identity of my own. I was brought up Egyptian Somali, but I wasn't sure which I was because I couldn't speak either language. I thought by speaking Welsh I would cement my own Welsh identity but then how do you define what being Welsh is? I don't think identity is about geography or language or colour. It's about what's in people's hearts.)

The actor Ali Yassine, half Egyptian, half Somali, has learned Welsh.

When exploring the idea of Welshness on her world tour in search of Welsh-speakers and learners, Pamela Petro was surprised to encounter the notion of Welshness by degrees:

If I've heard the phrase, Oh, he or she – usually he – is 'very Welsh' once on this trip I've heard it a thousand times. There seems to be a consensus among the Singaporeans that Eleri is just

116

a little 'more Welsh' than everyone else on the island. I can't imagine a more foreign notion. I would never think to call myself more or less American than anyone else I know. The state of being 'very American' is usually reserved for inanimate objects, like big cars and cheeseburgers . . . America, of course, is too plural to pin down to a specific national identity, and too powerful to worry much about it; Wales, on the other hand, is not only tiny but ever-defining itself so it won't wake up one day as England. Nonetheless, I have a suspicion that language lies at the root of the problem. And this is a problem. . . . Living with a linguistic sliding scale for the past century or more has created what I can only call an atmosphere, or a mindset, of comparison in Wales.

The notion of 'Welshness by degrees' has prompted comments from writers such as Carol Trosset, the poet Gwyneth Lewis, and the researcher Huw Lewis. It may well be that this trend is more likely to crop up within a lesser-used language community, where people react in a variety of ways to the influence of the majority language.

Oliver Davies and Fiona Bowie collected accounts of adult learners who had become Welsh-speakers in 1992 in the book *Discovering Welshness*. The contributors provide little information about technical problems when learning. These are people who have progressed to fluency, or very close to fluency and may not recall their early struggles with the language's idiosyncrasies. In addition they are learned people familiar with study, high achievers, who when determined are able to learn to speak Welsh despite the general availability of English. The accounts concentrate more on the change being able to use Welsh has wrought in them and the new worlds the language has uncovered, rather than providing details of the actual learning process.

While there is no clear definition of Welshness the contributors reveal that knowing the language produced a new sense of Welsh identity and a deeper understanding of the people and country, its traditions and history. Phyllis Kinney believes learning Welsh gave her life a focus it would not otherwise have had, and indeed while she remains unwaveringly American she has become part Welsh. She also ventures that learners from outside Wales may have something to offer their adopted country.

Identity is very closely linked with a sense of belonging, a notion that was important for Fiona Bowie:

> The warm, informal style of communication which I have come to associate with Wales contrasted starkly with the quick, sharp and competitive atmosphere, congenial in its own way, of Oxford academic life. 'Where do I live? Where is my husband from? His father, mother, grandfather, grandmother . . . ? I grew up in a village where I knew and was known. This knowing belonging and placing of people, their family history and ups and downs is paradoxically one of the homecomings in Wales. From my own village experience I am well aware that two or three generations go into the making of a 'local'. In a way, Welsh-speaking Wales is a village, interlocking networks of relatives and neighbours. As one of an itinerant tribe I do not belong or expect to belong in that way. Nevertheless, without sharing in a past which is rooted in Wales I can enjoy the stability which belonging to a small community engenders . . . I began to glimpse both the fun of speaking Welsh as a private language and the sense of acceptance into a small Welsh-speaking world that could follow . . . This Wales is as foreign to me as Germany, in many ways more so, but it is precisely this combination of otherness, together with a sense of belonging, which is my Wales. With the respect and awe with which we must always approach 'other people's dreams' it is all there waiting to be discovered . . .

Fiona has noticed that some incomers and learners born in Wales with English as their mother tongue even adopt a new identity, 'go first-language', exclusively mixing with Welsh-speakers and seeking work through the medium of Welsh. Some even change their names, play down any non-Welsh links and join the more radical Welsh language movements. Some of these learners may feel threatened by the less committed learner who can expose their adopted position. A short story by Toni Bianchi in *Discovering Welshness* illustrates this.

Un o ble dych chi?

Some learners however may feel uneasy with the Welsh interest in origins. Some, in particular those from outside Wales, cannot understand why the Welsh almost invariably ask, '*Un o ble dych chi?*' or '*O ble dych chi'n dod?*' when they meet someone for the first time. Some learners from inside Wales are quite sensitive about the issue too. R. Roberts wrote of his feelings on family origins in *Tu Chwith*. He believes that some Cymry Cymraeg are obsessed by family roots. He was brought up in a family in Swansea that had lost its Welsh language two generations earlier. However, the irony of the situation is that his 'Welshness' extended much further back than did that of some of the first-language Welsh-speakers who mocked his early efforts to learn Welsh.

The interest in roots in Wales can be traced far back in the history of the Welsh people and the preoccupation of Hywel Dda, King of Wales in the tenth century, with lineage. Such preoccupation with origins, however, may cause learners to experience feelings of 'anomie', a term psychologists use for the feeling of uncertainty about one's place and one's loyalties within the new language group. Learners are attracted by the new, but experience conflict because of emotional ties to the old, and can become anxious that too deep an involvement with the new culture will result in alienation from their own community. Students may fear loss of ethnic identity and insecurity about their place in both cultures. Some learners may never attain the first-language-like proficiency they desire because they may find that the reward of being fluent cannot compensate for the loss of identification and solidarity with their own first-language group, usually English. The practicalities of keeping pace with two social orbits may increase feelings of conflict. This situation is further complicated if only one member of a family chooses to learn Welsh and be integrated into Welsh society, particularly in an area such as south-east Wales where Welsh is not the language of the community. Such feelings of conflict, though, are not necessary. The two identities may be accommodated.

Dual Identity
Another contributor to *Discovering Welshness*, John Gillibrand, holds that he now has a dual national identity, Welsh and English. He is considered to be a Welshman by his English siblings, whereas other contributors to the book maintain that learning Welsh as an adult is

not sufficient to make one 'really' Welsh. For people living in multilingual, multicultural societies it is common to have a dual identity, for instance Cuban-Americans, Gaelic-Canadians, Chinese-Malay and German-Australians. These identities need not necessarily cause confusion, and could even help a person to bridge two language groups because of the association with either side. Learners can choose the aspects of Welsh identity they wish to embrace.

Anian (Ethos or temperament)

A particularly powerful contribution to *Discovering Welshness* is made by Mark A K Duggan. He believes in the central role of the language in supporting the Welsh identity but concedes that there is another Welshness, that argued for by historians Gwyn Alf Williams and Dai Smith, a conception of Welshness more appropriate to south-east Wales than to what Emyr Humphreys termed 'The Taliesin tradition' – in other words the erudite intelligentsia. This is a subject of great personal interest to me as I know that my ancestors had to choose between staying hungry in a Welsh language stronghold area and moving to find work where their family could eat – to an area where the Welsh language was forced to live so closely with English because of the in-migrants in the work place that it was losing ground rapidly. It is some sixty years since Saunders Lewis wrote *Yma bu unwaith Gymru* . . . (Here was Wales once . . .) describing the dereliction of Dowlais. Mark understands why these words provoked an angry response from the inhabitants of Dowlais and other valleys towns, who were and still are among the most materially deprived in south Wales. They could not be held responsible for the desolation of their environment or the gradual disappearance of the language and culture of their forebears. Many of these are people who may only know a few words of Welsh yet are offended if it is suggested that they are other than Welsh. They stake a resolute claim to Welshness:

It is unjust to stigmatise their inhabitants as half-breeds and turncoats, and still less as *bradwyr* (traitors), because they have lost, through no fault of their own, the language of their grandparents and all that went with it. Everything else about them proclaims, very loudly indeed, that they, too, are of the Cymry, and in the tale of the sorrows of Wales their lament is as great as any.

These are people who *feel* Welsh. This is why it is not surprising that in south-east Wales there has been such a boom in adults learning Welsh, for as Cennard Davies has commented, 'For the majority of non-Welsh-speaking valley residents, the language is not a remote phenomenon anyway, but a matter of relatively recent family history, with Welsh-speakers only two or three generations removed or even contemporaries in another branch of the extended family.'

These people have, then, what could be termed in Welsh *anian* (ethos or temperament). If their Welshness is limited linguistically, it knows no bounds emotionally, and when the emotions are stirred and people feel a sense of loss they are arguably more likely to persevere at restoring their family language than those who do so for more pragmatic reasons. They are keen that Welshness should be part of their future as well as their past. These are people whose emotions were stirred to action when it came to supporting an Assembly for Wales. David Balsom identified the '3 Wales' model in 1985, and despite fragmentation in the linguistic heartland the model remains broadly true:

- *Y Fro Gymraeg*, in the west and north, the linguistic heartland of Wales.
- Welsh Wales, the industrial heartland of the old coalfield with self-assigned Welsh identifiers despite substantial language loss.
- British Wales, the border counties, Severnside, the Vale of Glamorgan, north east Wales and south Pembrokeshire.

It is striking that in 1997 the area identified as 'Welsh Wales' voted with the heartland areas of Wales in favour of an Assembly. The area identified as 'British Wales' (which includes Cardiff) did not. It may well be that the preservation of the language will derive great benefit from the contribution of the increasing numbers of learners in Balsom's 'Welsh Wales' as the heartland continues to fragment.

We are not English!

'The Welsh-identified learner' does not always feel accepted in Gwynedd. Fiona Bowie describes how distressing it is for learners who have grown up in south Wales and who later move to Gwynedd to be regarded as 'English'. While she knows south-Walian learners who have succeeded in using Welsh in Gwynedd even professionally, she is aware of others whose knowledge of Welsh is inadequate and who are sceptical about real integration. According to Fiona, Welsh and English can be used as ciphers for 'insider' and 'outsider' and serve to distance incomers from locals, and learners from first-language Welsh-speakers. She has formed the impression that it is easier for learners to feel accepted in the southern Fro Gymraeg (Ceredigion, Carmarthenshire, north Pembrokeshire) than in Gwynedd, although both are traditional heartland areas.

The situation may not be as clear-cut as Fiona thinks, as a misunderstanding of the meaning behind the words *Saeson/Saesnes* (literally English man/English woman) in north Wales may have caused some confusion. The terms are used by Welsh-speakers in north west Wales to describe English-speakers and does not necessarily imply that they are not part of Welsh society. In fact it may even take some time for first-language Welsh-speakers who move into the area to be accepted as belonging in Gwynedd and to be spoken to in Welsh. Judith Kaufmann said that Emlyn, her partner, a first-language Welsh-speaker, had to persuade some locals in Rachub to speak Welsh to him when he first moved to the area.

On the basis of her research, Carol Trosset believes that while a small minority resent the intrusion of learners into the Welsh language community, the majority express approval of learners' dedication and progress.

Joker in the pack

Fiona Bowie is probably right in seeing the Welsh learner as the 'joker in the pack' who does not fit neatly into either 'English' or 'Welsh'. She notes, however, that the learner 'can play both cards'. Fluent Welsh learners, in particular, have the potential to play a crucial bridging role between Welsh learners and Welsh-speakers, as they have an understanding of both groups and may act as role models.

It could be helpful if tutors prepared learners for issues of culture and identity that they will almost certainly meet, so that they are not shocked and disappointed if they come across first-language speakers who – deliberately or inadvertently – create the impression that learners have no place in Welsh-speaking communities. It is also vital that learners do not become linguistically or culturally marginalised and remain in their own group, for the language development of those who do not use their skills with first-language speakers is unlikely to flourish. Gareth Kiff, a senior tutor at Cardiff University and an advisor to *The Big Welsh Challenge*, has noticed that the most successful learners are usually those who not only want to communicate with Welsh-speakers but also have a keen interest in Welsh culture. He views an interest in the media and Welsh culture as a distinct advantage and believes such learners are more likely to persevere, as the need to understand the culture and the whole concept of Welshness makes learning the language more authentic.

Would you like to find out more?
Oliver Davies and Fiona Bowie (eds), *Discovering Welshness* (Gomer, 1992)
Julie Brake and Christine Jones *World Cultures: Wales* (Hodder Headline, 2004)

Chapter 11
Snakes and ladders – life events

Annwyl Athrawes,
Dair wythnos yn ôl penderfynais y buaswn yn bod yn ferch dda. Roeddwn
am wneud y gwaith cartref i gyd yn ofalus – a mwy. Roeddwn am fynd i'r
dosbarthiadau i gyd. Trwy'r amser buaswn yn meddwl am y Gymraeg.
Efallai y buaswn yn edrych ar 'Pobl y Cwm' . . . buaswn yn seren y
dosbarth. Roedd syniadau eraill gyda bywyd.

Yn gyntaf roedd rhaid i mi ofalu am fy mam ar ôl ei llawdriniaeth.
Nesaf, roedd problemau gyda'r gath. Aethom ni â hi at y milfeddyg.
Ar ôl y driniaeth aeth y milfeddyg ar wyliau moethus tra fwyton ni fara
ac yfed dwr trwy'r mis.

Yna rhaid i ni ofalu am fy wyrion. Roedd peswch drwg arnyn nhw. Yn
fuan roedd peswch drwg arnom ni. Wedyn roedd pneumonia ar fy ngŵr
. . .

Fyddaf i ddim yn dweud wrtho chi am fy nhrafferthion i gyd. Mae
rhywbeth bach yn poeni pawb, meddan nhw. Ond nawr rydych chi'n
gwybod pam nad ydw i yn rhugl yn y Gymraeg.
Cofion gorau,
Zoë, y Ddysgwraig
Ionawr 2006

(Dear Teacher,
Three weeks ago I decided I would be a good girl. I wanted to do all
the homework carefully – and more. I wanted to come to all the
classes. I would think in Welsh all the time. Perhaps I would watch
'Pobl y Cwm' – I would be the star of the class. Life had different
ideas.

First of all I had to look after my mother following her operation.
Next there were problems with the cat. We took her to the vet.
After the treatment the vet went on a luxurious holiday while we ate
bread and drank water for a month.

Then we had to look after my grandchildren. They had bad
coughs. Then my husband had pneumonia . . .

I won't tell you all my troubles. Everyone has something small to worry them, they say. But now you now why I am not fluent in Welsh.

Best Wishes,

Zoë, the learner

January 2006)

Time

Zoë is still learning Welsh after a short break, but under such a combination of life events many learners give up because they cannot devote the time to attend class and learn *and* practise outside. Some do not restart, others give up for a time and then restart sometime later, often repeating the stop/start pattern many times before they become fluent. Adults have numerous commitments which may distract them from learning, so their road to fluency may include many peaks and troughs. Philip described this as a 'snakes and ladders' experience. Other aspects of individuals' lives, then, are closely linked with learners' progress when learning Welsh.

Some of the AWLP students were fast and successful language learners. Alan and Sally, for instance, progressed to *Defnyddio'r Gymraeg Uwch* within a few years and spoke with confidence. Others took far longer, often reporting a disrupted career of learning Welsh, with most having attended several courses in the past. Some of the students in the AWLP had been learning intermittently for over twenty years and, in one case, for more than thirty years. The WCC reported in 2005 that some learners made several attempts at learning before achieving success, and many of the successful students had attended an intensive course.

It is possible to learn rapidly and become fluent within a year. The winner of the 2008 Learner of the Year competition, Madison Tazu, had been learning on intensive courses for only ten months when she received her prize. Jen Llywelyn, author of *Welsh in a Year!*, gained fluency within a year. However, though both believe it is possible to gain a degree of fluency, they realise that there is always more to learn as absorbing a second language is an on-going process. It is essential for students who are unable to attend intensive courses, or cannot allocate much time to practise, to carry on learning as and when they can, as being exposed to even a small amount of language regularly will result in fluency eventually.

The Learner of the Year in 2008 was Madison Tazu, who seized every opportunity to use the Welsh she learned in class.

Every little helps

If the pressures of life mean you are no longer able to attend classes there are ways of keeping things ticking over until life is more stable and classes and regular practice can be taken up again.

Some tips for those who are under pressure:

- Try to do some Welsh every day even if it is only for five minutes.
- Learn one new word or phrase every day – have the word up in your kitchen or bathroom or office and collect the vocabulary in a small note book.
- Watch the news or weather forecast when possible on *S4C*. (Use subtitles if you are at an early stage of learning.)
- Listen to *Radio Cymru* and/or Welsh CDs in the car or when doing practical things at home.
- Try to use the Welsh you have at every opportunity.
- Buy *Lingo Newydd* and gradually work through the articles over two months.
- Have a novel for learners 'on the go' even if you only read a

few sentences a day.
- Try to use odd moments, e.g. on the station platform, waiting at the dentist, to read a little Welsh or learn vocabulary.
- Don't think of yourself as a failure who has given up but as someone who has had to take a temporary break.

Robert and Lucy Plane, professional musicians I taught occasionally over several years, made very fast progress despite often many weeks passing without a lesson because of their travels. They still keep up their Welsh by speaking at a Mother and Toddler Group and at their children's school. The birth of their third child meant they could no longer fit in time for lessons. However, as there is motivation to gain fluency and ready-made practice opportunities at school, it is highly likely they will eventually be fluent speakers.

Busy life styles
Welsh learners tend to have busy life styles. Learning the language tends to attract the committed and active rather than those who are short of something to do. Students on the AWLP were all occupied caring for families and had full or part-time jobs. Even Agnes and Philip, who were retired, had little spare time, as Agnes took responsibility for her grandchildren and Philip was involved in many other activities. Some students, such as Clare, travelled a long distance to work and this impinged on the time available for study and practice. Cathy, Sharon and Rees each attributed their lack of practice to laziness as well as their busy lives. However, the problem appears to go deeper than laziness, since these are conscientious people. Lack of confidence when using the language outside may be partly to blame, as well as tiredness, particularly on the part of those bringing up young children. Annabel noted in her journal, 'Conversation in a Welsh carol service' in 2006: 'I have recognised that when I am very tired (as was the case then), I struggle even more with understanding and word-finding and find the whole process of speaking Welsh very tiring, it requires a great amount of brain power!!'

Students at focus groups said they were wary of speaking Welsh when making arrangements for transporting children to school and other activities as they wanted to be absolutely sure that everything would go to plan and the children would be safe. They realised they could make the arrangements bilingually but sometimes the pressures of day-to-day living made this impractical. One of the first-language interviewees at the National Eisteddfod, Angharad, said that she knew several learners but that they frequently spoke English together because of the time factor.'*Mae bywyd yn brysur a thrio trefnu pethau yn anodd yn y Gymraeg.*' (Life is busy and arranging things is difficult in Welsh.)

In theory, students with children in Welsh-medium school or with a Welsh-speaking partner were at an advantage: even if the family spoke very little Welsh to them, they were exposed to the language at home, reducing the need to go out to seek Welsh-speakers in the community. In practice, however, unless a strategy is agreed, use of Welsh within the family may be pushed out as there is often a disinclination to speak in any second language to a close family member if this means changing the established language of the home.

Two of the intermediate students, Rees and Roger, were capable of attending an advanced course. However, Rees, who reads Welsh well and has a particularly wide vocabulary, lacks confidence in speaking Welsh and is very busy. Roger, who has a good command of grammar constructions and a fairly good vocabulary, is also content to remain at intermediate level on account of his busy lifestyle.

Philip explained that over the thirty years he has been learning, there had been many phases where he had conversed regularly in Welsh with his family and friends and acquaintances. However, he had been unable to sustain his good intentions for very long, partly because – as with other activities such as learning a musical instrument – he was not able to keep up the regular commitment. Other students attributed their chequered language-learning career to time pressures, the lack of opportunity to practise, having a baby, moving house, changing job, and bereavement. Annabel noted too that when another second language is in regular use there may be a temporary slowing down of the recall and use of Welsh:

At the time, we had a French lady staying with us and I was getting very confused with the two languages! The Welsh teacher was talking to me and I was responding '*Oui, oui!*' I think this is because I am a Welsh learner and the language is not consolidated in my brain. I learnt French up to 'O' level. Since the French lady has left, the confusion has lessened!

Lynne Davies reported that many questionnaire respondents in her study of learners' experiences said lack of time was a problem. She suggested that tutors try to integrate the Welsh language into activities already on-going in the students' lives, such as sport, music or activities with children. The tutor should look for occasions to guide each student as an individual into what would be helpful for them. It could even be worth setting individual, rather than class, homework for students who are not beginners. Many tutors are, of course, pursuing this route, but it may not be possible for students to find suitable Welsh-speakers in their immediate locality, particularly if their interests are not mainstream. Alice, a beginner noted:

Ideally, I need an interesting (possibly bilingual) activity that I can take a family member to also. We've just started horse-riding lessons together, for example, but I don't think any of the instructors would want to teach me in Welsh!

When will I be fluent?
Students often ask, 'How long will it take me to become fluent?' Clare asked this before I had even started the interview. This question is virtually impossible to answer as so much depends on an individual person's language-learning ability, motivation, intensity of instruction, prior experience in learning foreign languages, support from family and friends, the time available for learning and practising and the response of the local language community as well as on the level of fluency a student wishes to attain. The road to fluency is usually quite a long one. Adults sometimes expect too much too early on in the language learning process and become disappointed. Unrealistic expections often arise because family and friends of the learners make comments such as, 'You have been going every week for two years to Welsh and you are still not fluent.' This makes the learner feel a failure, yet the person who has made the comment has usually not learned a second language and has little idea what is involved.

The degree of fluency learners desire varies greatly. Some

learners are content to get by using Welsh with their families and friends for day-to-day matters but turn to English to discuss complex issues. However, others can only be satisfied if they can do everything in Welsh. In Chapter mentioned Andrea's disappointment, and her thwarted expectations which she attributed to the many language resource titles that promise fluency within a short space of time. Later I described how she bemoaned that she was not able to discuss complex issues in Welsh. This is quite a common reaction. Time investment is necessary in order to gain fluency quickly. As a result of expecting too much too early in the learning process students may become restive and discouraged. Others however are willing to practise simple conversations with children and adults and gradually build up to discussing more complex issues.

Dyfal Donc!

But why is everyone in such a hurry? Unless Welsh is needed to gain employment there is no reason why it should matter that it takes some time to become fluent. Is it not preferable to learn slowly and gain fluency rather than make great progress initially and then give up on it because it's not practical to keep up the time commitment? It is better for some people to be a tortoise than a hare when it comes to learning a second language well. Remember, in the fable it was the tortoise who won the race. You can read the story in Welsh, *Y Crwban a'r Ysgyfarnog* by Elin Meek..

Learn the Welsh saying:

'Dyfal donc a dyr y garreg.'
(Tapping persistently breaks the stone.)

Sandi Thomas, daunted by private study in the USA, enrolled on an WLPAN in Aberystwyth in 2000. Like June Barnes she soon realised that learning Welsh is not something that happens rapidly, indeed it may take a lifetime and is 'a tough hill to climb alone'. The realization of the time and hard work required to make significant progress may well play a critical role in decisions to drop out from Welsh classes. In fields such as sport and music, adults expect to work hard to achieve success, but inconsistently expect fluency in a second language to come about quickly. Judith Kaufmann commented, '*Beth mae'r pobl yn meddwl pan maen nhw'n dechrau dysgu iaith? Ei fod o'n digwydd heb waith?*' (What do people think when they start learning a language? That it happens without work?)

Ideally, intensive courses are the best option for helping learners to get to grips with the language and become fluent relatively quickly. Indeed some of the early pioneers in WfA believed that once a week classes should be abandoned and that all classes should be at least twice a week. However, there are those who have been unable to attend intensive courses have eventually become fluent by attending once a week over a long period. If the motivation to persevere is there, fluency will be achieved.

It is not just learners who need to persevere, though. Ann stressed, '*Rhaid i ni fel Cymry Cymraeg gofio i ddyfalbarhau. Dych chi ddim yn helpu pobl os dych chi ddim yn siarad Cymraeg â nhw.*' (We must remember to persevere as Welsh-speakers. You are not helping people if you do not speak Welsh to them.)

Opportunity

Linked with the time issue is opportunity to practise and use the language. There will always be fewer opportunities for learners to practise a lesser used language such as Welsh than a majority language such as English. In south-east Wales, for instance, Welsh is not a community language, but more a language of networking, so it was often tricky for the students in the AWLP to find opportunities to practise, particularly when their busy life styles were taken into account. Laura, who lived in a Welsh heartland area before coming to Cardiff, said she had practised in shops there, but such opportunities were quite rare in Cardiff. The younger the learner, or the newer to the area, the easier it is to build up a social circle of Welsh-speaking friends. However, Alice, who was fairly new to Cardiff wrote:

I am learning Welsh for pleasure, as an intellectual challenge and to learn more about this country adjacent to that of my birth. I do not *need* to learn Welsh for any particular professional or personal reason. I think these factors go some way towards explaining why I have difficulty in finding opportunities to practise speaking, listening and reading Welsh. I am new to Cardiff. I have no Welsh-based hobbies, and I do not encounter the language in use in any natural part of my existing home or work routine.

And Sioned, one of the younger participants, said it was hard to build up a Welsh-speaking social circle: she had so many friends already in the city who spoke only English, it was difficult to keep up two social circles. Some people can metamorphise and change their social circle and the language of their home, but the radical metamorphosis of a Bobi Jones is quite atypical. Walter Ariel Brooks from Patagonia stresses that learners have to create situations to use the language if they do not exist in the immediate environment. If learners do not use the language, they could well become wearied with learning as they will not see much fruit for their work. Walter said that he and his wife, Geraldine, have had to adapt their lives in Cardiff in such a way that they ensure they have regular contact with Welsh-speakers.

Walter's top tip

'Adapt your lifestyle to include regular contact
with Welsh-speakers if you do not already move
in circles where Welsh is spoken.'

Mas o'r bocs
Rachel Heath-Davies, director of the Centre for Teaching Welsh to Adults at Cardiff University, advises learners to 'get out of the box'. Do not always be looking in expected places for stereotypical Welsh-speakers. There may be some far closer to you than you think – for example, there may be a porter at work who would be glad to be your mentor and give you short bursts of practice on a regular basis. But do not wait until you are fluent. Use what you know straight away.

'Be prepared to find Welsh-speakers in unexpected places!',
says Rachel Heath-Davies.

Rachel's top tip

Use what you know **straight away**

Cardiff or *Caerdydd?*

In 1992 Oliver Davies recalled his youth in Cardiff, 'My teens were spent in Cardiff where (rightly or wrongly) it seemed that I was living in a kind of Welsh-flavoured England. Wales (though very close) was in a sense a foreign country.' Despite the increased Welsh ambience, as a result of the not insignificant growth in speakers and the prominence of bilingual signs following the 1993 Welsh Language Act, it is possible for the growing Welsh identity of Cardiff and its environs to remain unnoticed by in-comers and even by disinterested parties within the city.

Alan is certain that 'Cardiff has become more Welsh' over the last twenty years. And there have been comments to that effect in the press. Ifor ap Glyn, who returned to Cardiff after spending ten years in north Wales, was struck by the way Welsh is penetrating areas other than the media and education. He noticed that even the garbage lorries emit a bilingual message now and there is more chance of meeting Welsh-speakers in a restaurant or public house. Jon Gower, the television presenter, was surprised to discover that his local baker is learning Welsh. However, despite ubiquitous Welsh signage and successful events such as the St. David's Day March, it will take some time before the majority of Cardiff inhabitants know Cardiff as *Caerdydd*. At the turn of the Millennium, Peter Finch, Chief Executive of the Welsh Academy, commented that in Cardiff, 'Half of its population still think they live in the West Country and the rest don't care.' While this is clearly a tongue-in-cheek overstatement there is probably truth in his comment, 'Cardiff does not feel a very Welsh place despite the bilingual street signs and the willingness of the Halifax Building Society to take your money from you *"yn Gymraeg".*'

In 2001 the late Miles Kington was commissioned to write a promotional article for the Wales Tourist Board, in which he extolled the virtues of Cardiff as a cosmopolitan city offering international cuisine and a proliferation of impressionist paintings within comfortable proximity to England. Even the engaging description of his visit to the Museum of Welsh Life failed to indicate that Cardiff possessed a unique identity, linguistically or otherwise, as opposed to any other regional capital.

Cardiff/*Caerdydd* is changing slowly and it is still only the more determined of learners who search out opportunities to use Welsh in Cardiff and the surrounding area on a regular basis. Even in areas of Cardiff such as Whitchurch, where there are many Welsh-speaking families living in the same road, there is nothing resembling the almost exclusive community spirit that existed in traditionally Welsh-speaking areas, where the close-knit community was bound ever closer by Welsh language ties. Upwardly-mobile generations and the effect of migration mean that the old exclusive community is ebbing away in the Welsh heartland areas, and cannot be artificially fostered in the city. More clinical types of ties could replace the old closely knit communities as Welsh-speakers depend more on networking, even relying in some cases on electronic communication, rather than the immediate community.

Ultimately language is a social phenomenon, and learners need to find a domain, such as a Welsh society, a choir, a chapel, a sports club or a public house where they can practise their speaking skills or even just *listen* to Welsh, initially, in such a setting. It *is* possible for learners to practise successfully and progress to fluency in the more anglicised areas of Wales, even when they have no Welsh-speaking family or friends – like Liz Morgan, one of the 2001 finalists in the Learner of the Year competition. Liz stresses, however, that to do so, learners have to be particularly proactive in finding opportunities.

Gwen Awbery put forward a Welsh-speaker's angle on this matter:

It is difficult for Welsh-speakers to have opportunities to use Welsh in Cardiff and when they get together they may find it particularly stressful to have to accommodate learners. I would have to change my lifestyle completely if I wanted to speak more Welsh on a regular basis. Time is a factor for first-language speakers as well as learners.

Just one contact

As well as working on the linguistic skills in class and overcoming problems that arise in the community, learners need good time management skills and the resolve to seek out opportunities to use Welsh outside class. We are back to motivation being key to the whole issue. According to Zonia Bowen, one of the founders of *Merched y Wawr*, 'No, you can't learn any language without hard work and dedication. That is where incentive is important. If you are keen enough you will enjoy the effort and hard work, and the more languages you learn the easier it becomes to learn a new one.'

In 1978 Cennard Davies wrote a chapter on 'Some Learners' Problems', in which he discussed the vexed question of learners' difficulties when seeking to practise outside class. Cennard wisely advised learners to find one person initially: one sympathetic person who is willing to listen and guide you is worth more than a hundred who are clueless about how to encourage learners. Having such a person would help many learners to stay motivated when they are flagging. This advice was echoed by Alison Layland, a particularly successful adult Welsh learner. Ideally a person and a domain would help bolster the learner and accelerate their path to fluency. A mentor system has been used to a degree over the years in some centres, but if we were living in a perfect world where resources were no object it would be invaluable to every learner to be put in touch with a first-language speaker or a fluent second-language speaker as a mentor, who would have contact with the learner at least once a week. If the worst comes to the worst and you really have no one with whom to practise Dr Adrian Price suggests learners talk to their pets – and if you have no pet still speak Welsh out loud at home, or in the car, as it is so important to say what you are learning.

Meggan Lloyd Prys from Ohio married a Welshman, and won Learner of the Year in 2009, after learning for only two years.

Would you like to find out more?
Cennard Davies 'When you first start to speak: some learners' problems', pp 39-53 in Peter Finch (Ed) *How to Learn Welsh* (Christopher Davies, Swansea, 1978 – out of print but available in libraries)

Chapter 12
'I'm scared of what they say back' – anxiety and lack of confidence

Of recent years many scholars have stressed the place of anxiety as a hindrance in language learners' progress, and some would argue that anxiety plays an even bigger role when learners practise and use their second language in the community than in class.

Have a go!
Some students appear nervous and diffident generally. Although a great deal can learned by listening, if someone is usually very quiet and does not speak in his or her mother tongue, this does not bode well for language practice. All the AWLP students were leading active, responsible lives and not visibly anxious in other areas of their lives. However, they all either wrote about anxiety and lack of confidence in their journals or spoke of it at interview and in focus groups. They were all learners with high levels of education. Agnes volunteered at focus group, 'I'm scared of what they say back' as her reason for not using Welsh with Welsh-speakers at every opportunity.

Roger surely hit the nail on the head commenting, 'Conversation is the key. If a learner has confidence and understanding sufficient to carry out a simple conversation, the rest will follow.' Roger viewed language in a similar way to learning a musical instrument. Students have to know the scales before they play a tune. Similarly, learners need a basic knowledge of Welsh before they can start conversing outside class and then if there is enough confidence to keep at it, fluency will eventually follow. Roger viewed himself as lacking in confidence and attributed this mainly to time pressure as he has a responsible job and a young family. However, he commented that he was more confident than his wife, who is also a learner. His wife's diffidence has been very obvious when the family have been in France on holiday. His wife speaks some French but Roger knows only a little. When they need to converse with local French people his wife tells him what to say and he does not mind 'having a go'.

Being prepared to 'have a go' is often not linked to the learner's ability. Rees commented that his wife, who is also a learner but does not have the command of grammar or the vocabulary he has, is more confident than he is using spoken Welsh, even in her workplace, a bank. Similarly Sioned, who has no qualifications in Welsh, has the confidence to 'have a go'; her sister, an academic who has passed several examinations in Welsh, is not as confident as Sioned. But why won't some learners 'have a go'?

Taking risks and fancy dress

It could well be that those who are reluctant 'to have a go' are too concerned about accuracy and so they are not willing to take risks and make mistakes. Adults tend to be more reluctant to take risks than children: they often doubt their ability to learn and fear looking silly and being rejected if they make mistakes.

In the 1930s the psychologist Erwin Stengal compared adults learning a second language to a person wearing fancy dress. Erwin believed that adults often fear they will appear ridiculous. The adult learner may *want* to wear his fancy dress, but is inhibited by fear of mockery and criticism. The child, on the other hand, sees language as a form of play and enjoys wearing his or her fancy clothes. The more of 'these infantile characteristics' adults have preserved, the more easily they will learn a second language according to Erwin whose views are still quoted by contemporary scholars. Erwin's insights remind me of C. S. Lewis's comment, 'When I became a man I put away childish things, including the fear of childishness and the desire to be very grown up.' In other words it is the most adult among us who have lost the fear of seeming childish. It is certainly my experience as a tutor that the students who are willing to take risks and experiment with language – to the extent of making themselves look foolish – are often the more successful language learners in the long term.

Widespread lack of confidence

Lack of confidence was discussed at length at focus groups. In a questionnaire sent to students a few months after the focus groups, fourteen out of nineteen students disagreed with the statement, 'I am confident when I practise speaking or listening to Welsh.' The response was disappointing, especially as there were no beginners at this stage.

Several students volunteered that they had missed practice opportunities because of anxiety. Alan and Philip, who have particularly good oral skills, admitted to this and Sharon, not quite such an advanced learner, but capable of holding a conversation wrote in her journal:

> At Mother & Toddler today it was busy and I managed to speak Welsh to a few people. I am using it more with the children but the more I do the journal the more I realise how little I am making the most of the opportunities to use my Welsh. But it is very hard to summon up the confidence, which is definitely the biggest problem!

And Agnes wrote, 'I cannot cope with talking to people on the street.'

Intriguingly, Alice, the beginner, said she was not lacking in confidence to use Welsh outside class. Her main problem was lack of opportunity in her social circle – despite her limited knowledge she was willing to practise with first-language speakers at every opportunity. Alice had lived and worked in France for some years when she 'had to do everything through French'. Having had to work through a second language in the past is certainly good experience for a third-language learner, and it could explain why there are quite a few successful Welsh learners who have learned English as a second language.

Alice's attitude is the exception rather than the rule. Tutors who commented on the AWLP study realise that lack of confidence was a widespread problem for learners. Gareth Kiff thought this situation could be brought about in some learners who compare their progress in Welsh to their competence in their mother tongue.

I have referred more than once already to how important it is to wear badges to advertise Welsh skills. However, many students do not wear their badges. This may be partly forgetfulness, partly that orange does not go with what they are wearing, but many are afraid a Welsh-speaker may think they are better than they really are and try to carry on a complex conversation. It is this ambivalence again: the desire to practice but the fear of taking the plunge.

Sometimes learners feel strongly that first-language speakers are patronizing them and this undermines their confidence. When Craig Bohren opened the Learners' Tent in the 1978 National Eisteddfod he said he thought the word *dysgwyr* (learners) carries nuances of inferiority. He favoured the word *mabwysiadwyr* (adopters), as learners do not wish to be categorised as learners when they are able to use the language in the community. The highly-esteemed linguist Vivian Cook thinks that it would be better to call learners 'users' when they are able to hold conversations and function in the community as it becomes demeaning to call them learners. However, the word *dysgwr* continues to be used in Wales for learners at all levels, and first-language speakers may upset learners when they attach the label.

Sioned, for instance, reported feeling daunted on hearing Welsh-speakers saying, 'They are good but I could tell they were learners.' However, first-language speakers are usually just expressing surprise and admiration for learners.

Lack of confidence may also colour reactions linked with issues we looked at earlier, such as first-language speakers switching to English. Gwen Awbery pointed out that it is a very public act to use a second language and learners can feel crushed and and 'put-down' if first-language speakers stop using Welsh. Welsh-speakers' speed of speech and use of dialect and slang may cause anxious learners to lose their nerve and switch to English, instead of asking in Welsh for the sentence to be repeated. Identity issues may appear more problematic, too, to the anxious learner. However, this is something of a chicken-and-egg situation, as it is difficult to be sure with individual students whether anxiety triggers a negative reaction or whether particular circumstances trigger anxiety.

Several first-language speakers interviewed at the National Eisteddfod volunteered that learners had problems with *hyder* (confidence). Bethan from west Wales commented, '*Dyn nhw ddim yn ddigon 'ffit' yn y pentref. Mae Cymry Cymraeg yn cymryd y 'soft opsiwn'weithiau. Dylai dysgwyr ddim aros iddyn nhw.*' (They are not sufficiently forceful in the village. Welsh-speakers take the soft option sometimes. Learners should not wait for them.) Two other Welsh-speakers, Cerys and Gwenda said they themselves suffered from lack of confidence about their Welsh skills as both had periods when they had not used the language. Gwenda said this made her more sympathetic towards learners and she always practises with them at work. Cerys said she regained her confidence by attending a *cwrs gloywi*, a course to polish language skills for fluent speakers and advanced learners and thus became acquainted with learners. She stressed the need to keep using the language after course completion so that she will not lose confidence again. Sometimes the line between first-language speakers and fluent learners is not clearly demarcated in the case of a lesser-used language such as Welsh, and in these circumstances the two groups can help boost each other's confidence. Gwenda commented that it was easier for learners to persevere now than it had been in the past as there are so many more courses and social activies in place to help them move forward.

Ann, a first-language Welsh-speaker from Bangor, stressed the need for learners to be braver and venture to join a Welsh society such as *Merched y Wawr* or *Cymdeithas Edward Llwyd* so that they are immersed in the language. Idris from Port Talbot placed even more emphasis on immersion. He knows many proficient learners and always uses Welsh with them, but the time must come when they no longer view themselves as learners. '*Rhaid i berson gael ei sugno i fewn i'r gymdeithas Gymraeg – osmosis.*' (A person must be sucked into Welsh society – osmosis).

Gwilym from Wrexham believed that *hyder* was the learner's biggest problem. '*Mae Cymry Cymraeg eisiau cywiro nhw gormod. Rhaid i chi gywiro yn y ffordd iawn. Dylai Cymry Cymraeg gael mwy o amynedd.*' (First-language speakers want to correct too much. You must correct in the right way. First-language speakers should have more patience.) Gwilym said that there were people in his work-place who did not want to show that they spoke Welsh as they were concerned about the standard of the language skills.

Tutors' Views

As lack of confidence is such an issue all round it is interesting to discover WfA tutors' views on the issue. At a conference in 2007 forty-three WfA tutors were asked to sort thirteen issues ranked by fourteen learners as being the most hindering to their progress in using Welsh outside class. Before the tutors saw the students' ranking, over half of them chose 'lack of confidence' as being the main issue. In fact the first six statements chosen by the students were the same, though not in the same order:

Tutor Ranking
- *Diffyg hyder* (lack of confidence)
- *Cyflymder siaradwyr Cymraeg* (speed of Welsh-speakers)
- *Siaradwyr Cymraeg yn troi i'r Saesneg* (Welsh-speakers switching to English)
- *Cyfleoedd cymdeithasol yn Saesneg* (opportunity factor – social circle English)
- *Gwahaniaeth rhwng dosbarth a'r byd go iawn* (difference between the class and the real world)
- *Amser yn cyfyngu* (time restrictions)

Student Ranking
- Lack of confidence
- Opportunity factor – social circle English
- Welsh-speakers' speed
- Time factor – work and time commitments limit practice and study time
- Welsh-speakers turning to English
- Difference between classroom and the real world

According to Robert G. Newcombe, professor of statistics at Cardiff University, such agreement would be very unlikely to arise by coincidence.

Boosting learners' confidence, then, is an area for concentration on the part of professionals in the field in the future and an important message to be conveyed to all Welsh-speakers.

Needless anxiety
Some of the AWLP students wrote about feelings of anxiety that turned out to be unwarranted. Kim, for instance, wrote:

Heddiw, roedd rhaid i mi fynd drws nesaf gyda rhif ffôn. Doeddwn i ddim eisiau mynd achos fy mod i ddim yn teimlo fel yn siarad Cymraeg. Wel, es i ac wedyn dim problem. Mae'r dau ohonyn nhw yn

hyfryd – maen nhw'n aros pan dw i'n ceisio i ffindio'r gair cywir ac os dw i'n mynd mewn Saesneg am brawddeg, dydyn nhw ddim yn cario ymlaen yn Saesneg. Maen nhw'n mynd nol i Gymraeg.
(Today I had to go next door with a phone number. I didn't want to go because I did not feel like speaking Welsh. Well, I went and afterwards – no problem. The two of them are lovely. They wait when I try to find the right word and if I go into English for a sentence they do not carry on in English. They go back to Welsh.)

Strategies

In the focus group, Kim admitted she had sometimes crossed the street rather than meet a Welsh-speaker and face making conversation. However, by the end of the journal-writing, she realised that her attitude was changing and perseverance had helped build confidence:

Hyder (confidence) is not such a problem for me. If I make a mistake people will have to accept I'm trying. I've been continuing to speak Welsh to other parents and that's going pretty well – I definitely feel I'm understanding more. I was speaking to Carys *o'r Mudiad* (from the Movement – i.e. the nursery movement) the other day. Previously I have found her very difficult to understand but I was really heartened as I understood 85% and managed to say everything I wanted to . . . I definitely feel I've made a transition now – there are several people in school who now instantly speak Welsh to me, whereas three months ago I rarely spoke Welsh with them and if I did it felt unnatural and didn't last long . . . Last week I went to have coffee with a Welsh lady – this is someone who I meet on the road to school and speak Welsh for five minutes so I was quite daunted at the thought of an hour. However, it was very good – I understood the majority of the conversation and the conversation flowed because I fleetingly slipped into English for difficulties but made sure then to return to Welsh. Progress is being made!

By speaking mainly Welsh, but switching to English when there were difficulties, Kim has developed an effective strategy. Not all learners develop as Kim did and some are in danger of becoming professional dodgers who only feel able to cope in the classroom situation where they feel more secure, for as Kim stressed, *'Yn y dosbarth mae pobl yn siarad yn glir.'* (In class people speak clearly.)

In the USA, language learners sometimes undergo strategy training in preparation for language learning. In Wales we do not have the resources, as yet, for such a venture but learners could evolve their own strategies by keeping a journal and by so doing understand themselves and their reactions better. Joan Rubin, an expert in strategy training, who has worked in the field for over thiry years commented on some of the AWLP journal writers'entries. She thought they were crying out for strategy training. She stressed that they need help in defining more realistic goals, not just carrying on a conversation. They also need knowledge and practice in using conversational strategies, especially those used in holding one's place in a conversation. In addition they need strategies to overcome their fears and feelings of inadequacy. Professor Rubin believes such training would help them be more effective learners.

In Kim's mind, confidence is linked with first-language speakers' attitudes to learners:

> I went to *** and spoke Welsh to the owner and a parent from school. Both these women insist on answering me in English when I speak to them in Welsh. This used to make me feel very inferior and I would give up and speak English. However, I have noticed lately that in situations such as these I am persisting in Welsh and feel more able to take the attitude 'Well, shame on them for not supporting a learner'.

A pro-active strategy – an awareness that sometimes the problem is not with the learner but with the first-language speaker – could well help many learners persist when a Welsh-speaker turns to English. Welsh-speakers, of course, are more likely to continue using Welsh with learners who appear robust and confident than with those who seem particularly anxious.

Philip, who has been learning off and on for over thirty years, developed strategies to bolster his limited confidence. He asked his wife to commit to a schedule for speaking Welsh so that he would avoid continuing 'to drift like a rudderless ship':

> On a three day cycle – Day 1 – we have a Welsh conversation when we get up until it is time to get out and do our separate things. Day 2 – we chat if we meet up at lunchtime or, if we don't, at teatime. Day 3 – we share in conversation during the evening. Avril's thinking being that there will be a variety in terms of things pertinent to talk about – one doesn't get into too set a pattern and hopefully it will be quite relaxed.

Journal writing can help learners recognize and overcome their anxiety and it could be that if learners talked over such issues with tutors, and were given set phrases to use when problems arose in the community, many learners would gain confidence to use Welsh more.

One of the participants in a focus group at the conference for WfA tutors in November 2007 came to the conclusion, '*Codi hyder y dysgwr yw prif swyddogaeth y tiwtor.*' (Raising the learner's confidence is the main function of the tutor.) While there is great value in this view, as with any problem that arises for learners there is a great deal of truth in another conference delegate's comment, '*Os fydd y cymhelliant yn ddigon uchel mi wnân nhw ffindo ffordd.*' (If the motivation is strong enough they will find a way.)

Welsh-speakers need a greater awareness of issues that impact on learners and hopefully this book will help produce this. Yet at the end of the day the onus is on the learner to overcome and continue to use Welsh despite all obstacles. It is also worth noting that anxiety can be motivating, for, as with any task, fear of failure and looking silly may well inspire hard work.

Tips for anxious learners
- Learning vocabulary, even if only a few words a day. Having a wide vocabulary will build confidence.
- Listening is also a non-threatening way of learning and there are many programmes on *S4C*, something to everyone's taste that could help boost the learner's listening skills.
- Reading *Lingo Newydd*, a magazine for learners that appears

every two months and reading books written specifically for learners, will also help build confidence. Books for learners with notes and vocabulary lists range from 'chick-lit' to an anthology of poetry. A good place to start would be the novels of Bob Eynon and Pat Clayton and gradually build up to reading adaptions of Welsh novels in the series *Cam at y Cewri.*

• Writing a journal may help learners find out what situations trigger anxiety and develop a strategy to overcome these.

Listening and reading are helpful boosts to confidence as they make the learner more prepared to face the 'real' world, but for the learner who is really fearful, only facing the fear and using the language will help reduce the fear factor. There is everything to gain by venturing out to speak, and nothing to lose, apart from looking silly sometimes. And does that really matter?

All kinds of crafts and activities are now taught through the medium of Welsh. Here Zoë Pearce is learning batik.

Would you like to find out more?
Stella Hurd & Linda Murphy (eds.), *Success with Foreign Languages* (OU, 2005)
Go to www.gwales.com for details of books in Welsh for learners

Chapter 13
Dial o'r Diwedd!
My Journal

Why write a journal?

As I have subjected so many learners to writing journals I thought it only fair that they should be avenged and that I should give it a go myself. In May 2000 I decided to keep a journal when I went on a trip to Germany with my friend Jenny who teaches French and German to adults in the north of England. I followed this up with journals over the next two years when I went with Robert to Lübeck, Munich and Rüdesheim. As my German, once fairly fluent, was quite rusty I decided I would record all the practice opportunities on the trips. I felt this would help me understand how learners react when practising Welsh outside class. Don't panic! I am not going to reproduce the whole journal here. I am just giving you some snippets from sections that illustrate some crucial points about language learning.

Journal writing can help learners understand themselves and their reactions and may help them develop strategies to learn and use the language more regularly and more accurately. Increasing studies have shown that when individuals write about emotional experiences, significant physical and mental health improvements follow. It has been claimed that writing in an exploratory way raises self-esteem and self-awareness and that, as well as reducing anxiety and depression, writing boosts the immune system. Nowadays students are often asked to write their reflections on their learning. After the AWLP project several learners told me that, though the main purpose of writing their journals was to help me, the researcher, understand more about how language learners think, it also helped the learners to change attitudes they were unaware of before they wrote the journals. Several students said they had not realised how many practice opportunities they had missed, sometimes because of anxiety, until they recorded their experiences in their journals.

In the United States journal writing for language learners and tutors is quite common, as tutors and researchers study groups of language learners by asking them to contribute regularly to journals. There has been little work of its kind in the United Kingdom and very little in Wales. However, an interesting journal of a Welsh language learner, Marilyn Lewis in New Zealand, is recorded in Marilyn's book, *How to Study Foreign Languages*. Marilyn stresses the role of the tutor in her journal writing, although she believes that the tutor can do little if the learner does not have strong motivation:

> It seems to me that the teacher has quite a part to play in providing some motivation. Although the urge to learn must come from within, there is no doubt that being congratulated on one's progress is a great support. Learners don't often have the chance to choose their own teachers, but if they do, they should look out for one who is encouraging . . .

Marilyn found transferring her classroom skills to the community difficult:

> You can get exercises right when nothing depends on it, but when a whole lot of factors come into play in a real conversation then things are not so easy. The time factor is crucial. Most people want to finish a sentence in reasonable time, especially when someone is waiting to hear it. The ideas move faster than the language and, of course, you are taking part in a dialogue, not making a speech, so the other person's contributions have to be taken into account.

My journal – snippets

May 29th 2000

Today we visited Hameln en route to our base in Nachterstedt, a village in what was East Germany until 1989. We asked several people the whereabouts of the tourist office. However, as we searched we realised that our two sets of directions were in conflict. A lady emerged from an office and I asked her in German. She said *in English* that she would take us. She asked us *in English* about ourselves but we persisted in speaking German and asked her questions so that eventually she returned to German. We arrived at the tourist office and asked for details of the key places to visit. We were *answered in English* again but persisted with German the whole time when buying souveniers, establishing we had the correct video for use in the UK and working out our currency. We felt we were making progress. We saw a colourful statue of a rat on a postcard as we were leaving the office and I went back and asked where it was. They answered in German. They must realise that we are determined.

We were directed to the statue of the rat which is in the square by the *Hochzeitsgebäude* (Wedding Building). We combed the building and could not find it. Jenny asked an elderly man on a bicycle. He told us it comes out of the building three times a day, a type of *Glockenspiel*. We had just missed a performance. Jenny said '*Ach so,*' in response to his explanation, which made her sound like a first-language speaker. I kept trying to say '*Ach so,*' like a local from then on but it sounded contrived. We seemed to be holding our own in German when buying a snack and gifts to take home as the Germans were not turning to English in the shops. Is this because we had built up confidence or because they are not English speakers?

Hotel Schwann, Nachterstedt
We were welcomed *in English* at the hotel but insisted on speaking German. We kept up a German conversation with the waitresses at dinner but afterwards when we asked the manager about the whereabouts of the railway station and bus stop he insisted on *speaking in English.*

We went out in search of the station and found it quite easily using his clear directions. It looked disused so on our return we asked the manager where we could go on the line. He promised to get information from the internet by the following morning. He kept *speaking English* to us even though we spoke in German.

May 30th 2000
The manager appeared with the internet information at breakfast. We told him we speak German but he *continued to speak English*. He may have been afraid that we did not understand enough German to realise that we had to change trains. I pointed to the sheet and said '*umsteigen*' (change) in a clear voice. I tried to trigger a conversation about the weather but he had little to say, although he did respond in German.

Today we visited Brocken, the highest mountain in the Harz with the tour group. It was *difficult to understand* the conductor on the train when we asked about how long the round trip would take. He had a very *strong accent*. However, we did not ask him to repeat the information. I wonder why! I always tell learners to make it plain that they have not understood a first-language speaker and ask for the information to be repeated slowly. However, most of us do not really want people to think we have not understood the first time. We spoke German in the cafés and had short bursts of conversation with Germans. I had to pass a series of utensils to a German customer behind me. English-speaking visitors looked at me in awe! It was something of an ego trip! Really it is a reflection on the attitude of the British to using languages other than English abroad.

Even in Jakobistrasse, Goslar, Germany, people turn to English!

31st May, 2000

I thanked the manager for the information and told him we are going to Goslar. I asked him in German about the weather forecast. He answered in German. Afterwards I realise that I had used a type of spoonerism and said *Hervorsage* instead of *Vorhersage* for weather forecast. He smiled at me in a kindly sort of way. I felt stupid and wanted to tell him I really knew the word, but thought it would sound trite to do so. This reminds me of how learners tell me about making mistakes but think it seems petty to say that they knew the right version all the time.

We decided to catch the local train rather than take the optional coach excursion to Goslar so that we can have more opportunity to practice. We set out in good time for the train and called in at the

Spar shop to check that we were not expected to buy the tickets in advance. The employees were reassuring. They knew no English. However, when I said *auf dem Zug* for on the train *they corrected me forcibly* and say *im Zug*. Two mistakes in one hour – mortifying.

We confirmed that we had to change in Halberstadt with the conductress, who was very helpful and spoke to us in German.

At Halberstadt we checked again that we were going to the right platform and asked at the counter for information on trains to Berlin. It turned out to be £40 and four hours' journey with two changes so we decided against it. The woman behind the counter held up five fingers for the correct platform. This seemed *insulting* after we had conversed in German with her about the possibility of a trip to Berlin.

Two hours later we arrived at our destination, the UNESCO world heritage town, Goslar. It was difficult to find Jakobistraße, which is full of *Fachwerkhäuser* (half-timbered houses). Eventually we were directed there by a young lady who explained clearly in German but then asked us where we were from and immediately *turned to English*. However, I continued to speak German.

There were no problems in shops and cafés using or understanding German but in the museum an intense young man was asked to take us around and gave *very speedy complicated explanations, some of which we found difficult to understand*.

On the return train journey to Halberstadt we checked with the conductor again and found that our internet information was incorrect and there was no connection to Nachterstedt in time for supper, a meal included in our package deal. There was no alternative – we had to go back by taxi. We made sure in German the taxi was not a 'total rip off' before we got in. The taxi man was talkative which was what we needed but *we could not understand his accent*. I could only understand a word here and there so I responded to him but was never quite sure if the conversation was going the way he intended. Jenny was very impressed that I could follow him and was really surprised when I told her that I couldn't but was guessing the drift from odd words I was catching.

April 2001 Visit to Lübeck with Robert
The language practice opportunities in Lübeck were far greater than on our trip to the Harz. The Baltic coast is not an area of Germany

that attracts British or any other English-speaking tourists. We broke the German-only rule at the station as the complicated price ranges and the trains on which special offers can be used are difficult enough to follow in a first language. Apart from these we spoke German the whole time and received many compliments.

Indeed by the time we visited the seaside at Travemünde, we were so used to using German that in the fish and chip café I spoke naturally to Robert in German and caused some embarrassment.

'*Keime,*' I said in a stage whisper on the third splutter.

Immediately the pale-faced man in the yellow fleece leaped to his feet and clutching his handkerchief headed for the *tŷ bach* (toilet). I had forgotten I was in Germany. '*Keime*' – germs in German – is a word I tend to use at home when someone coughs, sneezes or splutters in an eating place. Most people at home would be clueless as to the meaning. If they were to understand they would probably take no notice anyway. Our unhygienic companion returned in a few minutes and settled down to gobble omelette and chips, then with a furtive look in our direction made a hasty exit. I felt a bit ashamed of myself but could not help being amused.

There were no problems persuading people to speak German to us in Lübeck and the surrounding area. There were problems with accents sometimes but we just tried to keep the conversation flowing and smiled a lot on these occasions. Again, it is interesting that we did not say that we could not understand. Occasionally I could not bring vocabulary to mind. This was particularly frustrating in Bremen, when I wanted to tell a rotund little man with a red nose that I was not superstitious, as he pressed me to clutch the leg of the donkey on the statue of the *Bremer Stadtmusikanten* (Bremen Town Musicians) so that I would return to the city. I could only bring to mind the Welsh word, *ofergoelus.*

October, 2001 – Visit to Munich with Robert

I attended a conference in Munich with Robert. We were greeted at our apartment by the proprietor, a slim, middle-aged woman with the most amazing accent. She said *Na Ja* after almost every sentence. She greeted us in English but when she realised that we were happy to switch to German seemed relieved and spoke to us in German for the rest of our stay. We gradually got used to her accent.

Everywhere we went – shops, cafés, museums we spoke German and all the responses were in German. Why was it so much easier to sustain a German conversation in Munich than it was in the Harz last year? There must be many Germans who speak English in the city and yet they continue to sustain German conversations with me. Could this be because I appear more confident now as there have been three trips to Germany over the last eighteen months? Is it something in the learner's demeanor that causes the first-language speaker to turn to English? It is difficult to be sure on such a short visit but I strongly suspect that is the case.

What did I learn from my journal?
The main problems, ranked in order of importance:

- German speakers turning to English.
- Germans do not want to speak to us in some situations.
- The accents/dialects of German speakers.
- The speed of German speakers' speech.
- Inability to hear because of background noise.
- Condescending attitude of some Germans.
- Lack of confidence triggered off by mistakes.

Lack of confidence was high on the list of learners in focus groups but it was not a significant problem for me. I was rather disappointed when I realised I had made mistakes but I saw them in a constructive way as part of the learning experience. My main problem was *frustration in getting Germans to speak to me.* They wanted to practise their own English and sometimes they did not want to engage in conversation. This, of course, is not necessarily a problem specific to language practice. Some people do not want to engage in conversation with strangers on public transport and in cafés.

The *accents and use of dialect* were frustrating as well as the *speed of speech.* I did note as significant that when I did not follow because of speed or accent I did not ask the speakers to repeat unless the information was essential. Presumably, I do not want people to realise I have not understood. However, I am always telling learners not to worry about this, and to ask for material to be repeated whether it is because of a problem with speed, dialect, accent or just failing to hear. The condescending attitude of the lady who lifted up five fingers was annoying but we did not experience this often.

I assumed that Germans were speaking English because they needed the practice rather than because they thought my German was inadequate. However, I think the hotel manager wanted to be absolutely certain that I understood his comments and so spoke English. I thought this was significant. The learners I have studied tend to assume first-language speakers change to English because they expect that the learner's Welsh is inadequate. One of the learners wrote that he felt the same way in France, and although his knowledge of French is on a par with my German, he thinks the French turn to English because they see his French as inadequate. This thought did not occur to me when I was struggling to persuade people to speak German to me. The learner in question speaks Welsh very well apart from an obviously English accent. Presumably his French accent is also 'English' and this may account for the lack of acceptance.

We are looking at two different situations here. Everyone in Wales can speak English (with the exception of pre-school monoglot children), whereas only some Germans are fluent in English. Welsh-speakers are not keen to practise their English. However, the reason for the different reaction, I believe is the level of language ability I have in German. Even though I am out of practice I have no difficulty following day-to-day conversations if I can hear clearly and am not hindered by a strong accent. If a learner from a German class, who had only learned the basics, had tried to communicate in the situations I found myself in I believe they would have become very daunted. The tendency of the Germans to turn to English and to speak too quickly for learners would have disappointed them. In addition when faced with external factors such as background noise they may well have attributed their lack of understanding to their own inadequacies. A language learner would need to be very determined to persuade English-speaking Germans to speak to them slowly and clearly in the German language in order for them to practise the skills they have mastered in the classroom.

The act of writing the diary has been an extremely useful one in helping me to understand the problems encountered by learners. I will be more sympathetic in future when learners tell me that they were unable to initiate conversations with Welsh-speaking acquaintances. On past visits to Germany I have noticed that Germans want to speak English but the act of recording these occasions made it clear how frequently it happens. I will also be more understanding when learners say that they have to double-check in English about crucial matters of arranging times for children to be collected etc. The one occasion when I appreciated a double check was at the railway stations.

It also came to light that Jenny and I experienced feelings of *competitiveness*. We each thought the other was using expressions that were 'more German' or that the other was sounding 'more German'. Interestingly, I read about this happening afterwards in some of the tutors' journals in the States. While anxiety can be a hindrance to language students, it can also be a boost and give incentive to learners to struggle more. Jenny and I found the level of anxiety and competitiveness we experienced constructive, as it spurred us on to increase our vocabulary and learn colloquial expressions.

The trip and the journal keeping were a valuable language boosts for Jenny and me. We learned such impressive expressions as *Schickie Mickies* – Yuppies – and now feel generally more confident using the German language.

The four main lessons learned were:

- Insist on using the language you are learning whatever the first-language speaker does
  Always ask if you do not understand a word or phrase or if unfamiliar dialect or slang is used
- Ask the speaker to speak more slowly or repeat if necessary
- Don't worry about mistakes. Just enjoy the experience.

Would you like to find out more?
Marilyn Lewis, *How to Study Foreign Languages* (Macmillan, 1999)

Chapter 14
Ymlaen! (Forward)

Re-inventing the wheel

So where do we go from here? We have heard of learners' experiences and Welsh-speakers' reactions. We have established that motivation is central to success, and and we have received useful advice from tutors and others on how to help learners stay motivated. Hopefully, both learners and Welsh-speakers will develop strategies as a result of this book and be able to communicate more effectively. However, in one sense I feel that I have been reinventing the wheel. So much of this has been said before. In 1978 Cennard Davies wrote a chapter covering the issues we have looked at in depth and offered wise advice to learners. Also a variety of badges have been available for learners over the years. However, there is still not widespread appreciation of learners' needs among Welsh-speakers, as there has not been enough awareness-raising and marketing. Five out of eighteen of the Welsh-speakers said they did not know any learners and had never spoken to one.

In the 1970s, as the number of learners increased so did the realisation of the need to integrate them into Welsh life, socially and culturally, as well as providing an opportunity to practise new linguistic skills. A Welsh Office report in 1976 on adult Welsh learners noted that, with the best of intentions, Welsh-speakers may turn to English in the mistaken belief that they are displaying kindness, or some may make it obvious (thoughtlessly or unintentionally) that the learner's Welsh is halting and slow. The writers recommended that second-language teaching be supported by a campaign to persuade Welsh-speakers throughout the country to play an understanding and helpful part in supporting those of all ages who are learning the language. Suggested initiatives that would help towards this objective included a badge to be worn by those willing to converse with learners, and notices in places where there would be opportunities for them to practise. The fundamental need emphasised in the report was to awaken the awareness of Welsh-speakers to the growing importance of the learner in the struggle to strengthen the language.

It was particularly difficult for learners to practise in the more anglicised areas as there were fewer opportunities in daily life, and it was recommended that learners visit Welsh-speaking areas, and that friendships with Welsh-speaking families in their own locality be arranged. In addition it was recommended that Welsh-speaking organisations such as *Merched y Wawr* provide for learners. It was envisaged that new clubs specifically for learners be established where Welsh could be used at a level appropriate to learners.

Sounds familiar? How far have we moved in thirty years? Yes. Progress has been made. CYD and the *Mentrau Iaith* have done excellent work in integrating Welsh-speakers and learners, as have societies such as *Merched y Wawr*, and there are certainly many places for learners to practise their skills all over the country. Plans are on-going in the new centres for WfA to bring about more integration with Welsh-speakers and provide mentors. S4C have provided many useful programmes for learners and helped raised awareness amongst Welsh-speakers of learners' needs.

Marketing
However, far more awareness-raising is needed. Does every Welsh-speaker realise how much help and support learners need? Phyllis, one of the interviewees at the National Eisteddfod, claimed she did not know any learners. But in a subsequent discussion it transpired that she knew Philip, one of my students who is close to fluency but it had never occurred to her to speak to him in Welsh.

A media campaign to make it absolutely clear to Welsh-speakers that learners need their help could change the whole situation. *The Big Welsh Challenge* is already encouraging Welsh-speakers to be mentors, but many still see this as something for learners or for others, not for *all* Welsh-speakers. Everyone should support learners as the language is for all of us – *Iaith Pawb*.

Nid yn null y tân siafins (not with transient enthusiasm)
Professor Bobi Jones has stressed on many occasions that intervention from Welsh-speakers is vital but it has to be in the heart and not with 'transient enthusiasm'. Do they really want to help learners? They must be persuaded to see language survival not just for campaigners but the responsibility of every Welsh-speaker regardless of age,

ability or language background. Help for learners is as crucial for the future of the language as were the language campaigns in the 1960s. In fact Bobi has predicted that the fortunes of the Welsh language could change if language protestors were also to give one hour each week to provide learners with much-needed conversation practice.

Ond fy ŵyr hyd yn oed y protestwyr mae ewyllys barhaol y bobl yn unig i'wneud' drostynt eu hun sydd yng nghanol Addenill yr Iaith. Dim arall. Ac y mae gweithredu effeithio yn golygu bod y Cymry Cymraeg rhugl mwyaf brwd yn estyn llaw cymdeithas – yn benderfynol, yn drefnus, ac yn barhaol i'r Dysgwyr. Nid yn null y tân siafin, ond yn sefydlog. Rhythm gwahanol sydd ei angen i'r dyfodol. Gyda'i gilydd y maent yn ffurfio'r Adennill.'

(Even the protestors know that the people's enduring will to take action themselves is central to language renewal. Nothing else will do. To effect this, the most enthusiastic fluent Welsh-speakers must extend a sociable hand to learners – in a determined, orderly and enduring way. Not with transient enthusiasm, but consistently. A different rhythm is needed for the future. Together they can bring about renewal.)

Do Welsh-speakers realise that by giving even one hour a hour a week to practise with a learner they could help increase the numbers of fluent Welsh-speakers in Wales by the census in 2011? Television programmes in Welsh and English where learners discuss their experiences would help Welsh-speakers understand the issues.

Marketing is one of the key issues. In Catalonia a successful marketing campaign to promote the use of Catalan is on-going. The image of the campaign is a mechanism consisting of a set of chattering plastic teeth which symbolises the language and which has to be given a boost by winding it up so that it walks. Obviously if it is not given this boost, it stops. The idea is that everyone should give Catalan a boost so that its use does not stop. This image has become the campaign's mascot and after a vote among viewers of the *Televisió de Catalunya* programme *El Club*, it was called *La Queta* (the diminutive of *boqueta* or little mouth). In the course of the year, 122,000 units of *La Queta* were distributed. The campaign's mascot has become an icon and a character loved by most of society and

La Queta, mascot of the campaign to boost Catalan.

recognised by just about everyone. In a variety of forms *La Queta* was present at the most significant events throughout Catalonia, whether parading through the streets of towns as a traditional *gegant* (giant), taking part in Carnival floats or as an Easter figurine, etc. Her image was also adapted or characterised in a range of recreational, festival and sports contexts. The advertising launch of the campaign was also reinforced by merchandising which maintained her presence beyond the three weeks the media advertisements lasted. This included informational and promotional material such as leaflets, posters, stickers, bookmarks and balloons which were widely distributed throughout the region. The advertisement for the campaign included a song with lyrics and music featuring the campaign's slogan and three messages:

> *I'm not shy about speaking,*
> *I speak freely,*
> *And when I start,*
> *I speak in Catalan.*
> *I'm not shy about speaking,*
> *I speak freely,*
> *And if I make a mistake,*
> *I start again.*
> *Give Catalan a boost.*

This song has become a hit with young people. It can be downloaded free of charge as a ring tone for mobile phones along with wallpaper.

Wales could lead the world
The Welsh language is a leading example of reversal of language decline and learners have played and will play significant roles in this exciting time for Wales. But this is no time for complacency. A vast injection of funding is needed to promote the use of Welsh and to raise the awareness of the needs of learners. Tutors have a good understanding of learners' needs but their needs are only gradually becoming known to Welsh-speakers. Wales is bursting with talented tutors who could be leaders on the world stage. We have so much to offer other countries who are setting up intensive language courses. There has been a tendency to shrink back and lack confidence in the past about what we can give to other nations.

If more work were done to promote the use of Welsh and support learners in their efforts to use the language Wales and WfA could take a major place in language promotion globally and make a valued contribution to addressing difficulties faced by second-language learners, particularly those of lesser-used languages world wide.

I am ending this book with advice for learners who wish to become fluent; for Welsh-speakers on how to help them; and some innovative policies for the promotion of use of Welsh by learners outside class that could be debated by public, educational, voluntary and commercial bodies.

Twelve Tips for Learners who are aiming for fluency
- Practise as often as you can and start from day one of your course.
- Find at least one first-language speaker to help you. If this is impossible practise with a CD.
- Evolve a strategy if you are practising with a relative at home or a friend you meet regularly. In the early stages spend a short time e.g. three minutes each day at meal times and gradually build this up as you learn more.
- Do not worry about mistakes. See them as part of the learning process and try to laugh at them.

- If you do not understand what a Welsh-speaker says, ask them to repeat; '*Eto, os gwelwch yn dda*' (again, please) and ask meanings of any words that are not clear to you: '*Beth yw . . . yn Saesneg?*' (what is . . . in English?)
- Ask Welsh-speakers to speak slowly if you are not following them: '*Araf, os gwelwch yn dda. Dw i'n dysgu Cymraeg.*'
- Insist on speaking Welsh even if the Welsh-speaker turns to English. Only switch to English for a short while, to make an arrangement, for example, and then return to Welsh.
- If at all possible belong to at least one group where you can use your Welsh regularly e.g. a scrabble club or a choir.
- Watch as much Welsh television as you can and listen to *Radio Cymru* as often as possible. Do not worry if you do not understand early on in your learning as it will be useful for you to hear pronunciation and intonation in Welsh.
- Read as much as possible including websites for learners. Start with simple articles in *Lingo Newydd* and move on to novels for learners. Read out loud as often as you can.
- Keep a journal about your experiences learning Welsh and a small vocabulary book. You only need to spend a few minutes each day on the journal. Start this in English and gradually

Welsh-language Scrabble has proved a very popular way to practise the language

move into writing in Welsh. Note any new words and idioms in the vocabulary book and look at it in odd moments regularly, e.g. while waiting for the kettle to boil. Keep it with you always, in a bag or pocket, and always take it when you go away.

- Never think of giving up even if you are going through a time of pressure and stress. Keep ticking over until the time comes when you can pay more attention to developing your language skill.

Twelve tips for Welsh-speakers on how to help learners

- Always use Welsh with learners you know. If they are beginners, keep it very simple and try to teach them a new word or phrase every time you meet.
  With learners who are able to converse, do not switch to English, as this will undermine their confidence. Even if the learner is tempted to switch to English, insist on speaking Welsh, only using English for anything complicated – and then return to Welsh.
- With family members or close friends have a regular slot where you speak in Welsh, building up the time as the learner increases in knowledge.
- Speak more slowly and clearly than usual.
- Do not use dialect or slang with beginners, but with learners who are able to converse teach some vocabulary and language patterns used in your locality.
- Always encourage learners, and do not correct every mistake as this hinders holding a natural conversation.
  Stress the importance of correct pronunciation and intonation with learners, and help them by repeating words they find difficult to say.
- Wear a badge that indicates you are a Welsh-speaker.
- Familiarise yourself with the course books used in classes so that you are aware of the language patterns learners use.
- If you belong to a Welsh society, such as *Merched y Wawr*, think of ways of including learners in your meetings, or even of running an event specially for them.
- If you live outside Wales, advertise in the local paper, on a

notice board at work, or on a blog that you are willing to practise with learners.

Innovative policies that could be adopted/adapted by public, voluntary, education and commercial sectors

- Pre-course preparation for learners – how to practise classroom Welsh.
  Training for Welsh-speakers provided by the six National Centres on how to help learners
- National Language Campaign via *S4C/Radio Cymru*/BBC/ITV– encourage Welsh-speakers to be proactive about helping learners.
- National Assembly – commission research culminating in a handbook for Welsh-speakers with advice on how to practise with learners. For beginners, give examples of the registers used in the past, present, future and conditional, examples of dialect forms and main areas of problems with pronunciation to be addressed. Include tips from professionals in other areas such as ESL – experts in the States and Canada who have worked closely on issues affecting learners outside the classroom.
- Language board supply badges for all (3 badges per person to allow for damage and loss) all Welsh-speakers wear badges, *not just* in the workplace so that everyone knows who is who. All learners wear badges at all times. Instigate a national media campaign to ensure the success of this venture, a campaign akin to the one in Catalonia.
- Expand the mentor system on the lines of *Voluntaris per la llengua* in Catalonia.
- Expand the informal activities for learners. *Cynllun pontio* should be available in all classes all over Wales.
- Cafés, restaurant, pubs and shops advertise when they are willing to speak to learners.
- Commission a national survey of all learners and first-language speakers – asking what activities they would like to participate in to practise their Welsh e.g. sports, walks, bike riding, horse riding, or cultural – discussion of books, attendance at plays, concerts. museums, or crafts – knitting,

making jewellery etc. Employ an officer with experience in WfA in each centre to implement results.

- Media to film actual lessons, not simulated, on a weekly basis, to familiarise Welsh-speakers with what goes on in classes.
- *S4C* and *Radio Cymru* to broadcast quizzes for learners and dramas/operau sebon performed by advanced learners.
- Cafés and shops to welcome learners by advertising their willingness to speak Welsh to them.
- Arts Active to sponsor learners to perform simple plays in venues such as Level 3, St. David's Hall, Cardiff.

I am giving the last word to the pioneering Welsh
language enthusiast, Emrys ap Iwan:

'Os lleddir yr iaith,
fe'i lleddir yn nhŷ ei chyfeillion.'

(If the language dies [literally 'is killed'],
it dies in the house of its friends)

Abbreviations

AWLP	Adult Welsh Learners' Project
DELLS	Department for Education, Lifelong Learning and Skills
ELWa	Education and Learning Wales (In 2006 taken over by the Welsh Assembly Government)
HMI	Her Majesty's Inspectors
ULPAN	An intensive course in the Hebrew language and culture. *Ulpana*, the original term, is an Aramaic word that could be translated teaching, training or studio.
UNESCO	United Nations Educational, Scientific and Cultural Organization
WCC	Welsh Consumer Council
WfA	Welsh for Adults
WJEC	Welsh Joint Education Committee
WLB	Welsh Language Board (In 2006 taken over by the Welsh Assembly Government)
WLPAN	Intensive Welsh classes were named WLPAN in 1973
WTC	Willingness to communicate

Welsh terms

CYD	A society that aims to bring Welsh-speakers and learners together to socialize. Literal meaning: 'together'.
Cyd-adrodd	Group recitation
Cymdeithas Edward Llwyd	A Welsh natural history society
Cymdeithas yr Iaith Gymraeg	The Welsh Language Society
Cymmrodorion	A Welsh society for those interested in Welsh literature and culture
Cymry Cymraeg	Welsh-speaking Welsh people
Cynghanedd	The strict metre which forms the basis for much Welsh poetry
Cynllun pontio	A scheme that offers learners opportunities to practice with first-language speakers at the end of the lesson in the classroom

Dysgwyr	Learners
Eisteddfod	Festival of the arts
Gorsedd	A bardic order that admits those who have made a substantial contribution to Welsh language and culture. Literally means throne.
Menter Iaith	Language Initiative. A *Menter* is a local organisation that offers support to communities to increase and develop their use of the Welsh language.
Merched y Wawr	A society for women similar to the Women's Institute in other parts of the UK, but run through the medium of Welsh. Literal meaning: 'Women of the Dawn'.
Mudiad Ysgolion Meithrin	Welsh-medium Nursery Schools' Movement. An *'ysgol feithrin'* – the m is mutated – is a Welsh-medium nursery school
Nosweithiau Llawen	Entertainment evenings
Sianel Pedwar Cymru/S4C	Channel Four Wales
Ti a Fi	Mother and Toddler groups. Literal meaning: 'You and Me'
Urdd Gobaith Cymru	Organisation set up in the 1920s to encourage young people to speak Welsh in leisure time, sports activities, etc.

Some useful websites for learners

www.bbc.co.uk/wales/learnwelsh

www.bbc.co.uk/wales/colinandcumberland

http://www.bbc.co.uk/wales/learnwelsh/bigwelshchallenge/

www.bbc.co.uk/wales/catchphrase

www.gwybodiadur.co.uk

www.radioacen.co.uk

www.geiriadur.net

www.acen.co.uk

www.s4c.co.uk/cymraeg

http://www.cardiffhigh.cardiff.sch.uk/~mgd/index.html

http://www.madog.org/

http://cymrugydnerth.com/topics/educationandskills/wfasub/welshfor
   adults/learners/usefulcontacts/?lang=en

www.saysomethinginwelsh.com

Photo credits:

All photos by the author, except:

Caroline Hamilton (p. 15)(used with permission)
Chris Rees (p. 34)(used with permission)
Students on first WLPAN course (p. 35) (© Western Mail)
David Crystal (p. 41) (used with permission)
Tanni Grey-Thompson (p. 87) (used with permission)
Ali Yassine (p. 116) (used with permission)
Meggan Lloyd Prys (p. 136) (© Twm Siôn Cati)